Presente

Rise Write

By

Katy & Keith

Date

12-03

Coffee Break
Devotions
Cappuccino

An Invigorating Blend of Reflections
and Inspirations to Energize Your Day

HB
HONOR
BOOKS

07 06 05 04 03   10 9 8 7 6 5 4 3 2 1

Coffee Break Devotions: Cappuccino
An Invigorating Blend of Reflections and Inspirations to Energize Your Day
ISBN 1-56292-918-6
Copyright © 2003 by Bordon Books
6532 E. 71 Street, Suite 105
Tulsa, OK 74133

Published by Honor Books
An Imprint of Cook Communications Ministries
4050 Lee Vance View
Colorado Springs, CO 80918

Developed by Bordon Books

Manuscript prepared by Rachel St. John-Gilbert

Introduction

✺

When your go has gone and your up is down, it's time to stop and take a moment to reconsider and recharge before you head back out at breakneck speed. That's what a coffee break is for and that's the purpose of *Coffee Break Devotions: Cappuccino*—to take time to think about the important things of life and to consider new, more fruitful ways of living a life that counts.

With coffee in all kinds of flavors and forms, coffee breaks have never been more pleasurable. So kick back with a cup of your favorite blend, done your favorite way; and enjoy these coffee break sized, upbeat meditations. Then energized, you can speed up into hyper-drive and move out in life-changing ways that *really* set your world in motion!

*I shall light a candle of understanding
in thine heart, which shall not be put out.*

Getting Out of the Rut

I t's easy to feel trapped by our circumstances. The older we get, the more elements creep (or come bounding) into our lives—career, spouse, mortgage, kids, and all that accompany these "additions," from having to fix major appliances to the application of braces and the ensuing mental, emotional and physical demands. While there is joy in work and family, the complexity and responsibility can be overwhelming, especially when one is feeling discontent with a job, a home, or any other significant aspect of life. Sometimes making a change is as simple as making a decision and acting. Other times, because of finances and obligations, we lie awake at night trying every scenario possible only to realize we must continue on the same path.

Maybe a change of locale is possible and necessary, but sometimes a change isn't realistic, feasible, or even right. If a change isn't in order, God will help us find peace within our circumstances. Pay attention to your thoughts and attitudes. Make small changes in areas of your life that aren't as far-reaching. Don't forget to give yourself time to unwind and rest. Constant tiredness can warp the perception of the greatest optimist.

Oftentimes when we think we need a change, we only need a good night's sleep.

A heart at peace gives life to the body.

PROVERBS 14:30

I wished to live deliberately, to front only the
essential facts of life, and see if I could not
learn what it had to teach, and not, when
I came to die, discover that I had not lived.

The Lost Art of Silence

Stimulus hits us at every turn. There's hardly a place we can go where someone isn't sending a message. "Buy! Save! Win! Act now!" We can't even breathe easy inside our own homes, with telephone solicitors pleading through irritating scripted appeals. This constant distraction robs us of our thoughts, our sleep, and our peace—the very heart of our lives.

In this instant-info, global society, people need a break. Some of us have become so accustomed to receiving voices, music, images, and words that we no longer know and perhaps aren't even comfortable with the idea of silence. Is your only time of quiet when your head hits the pillow at night? Do you know your own thoughts? Can you relish a few moments without "tuning in"?

Many people have taken to living by their "Caller ID" boxes to achieve some level of control when they are trying to have a life at home. Whatever you do, take time for quiet. A quaint coffee shop off-peak (where you won't run into anyone you know), a walk through a gallery or park, or a drive to the mountains or sea. And don't touch that radio dial—that is, until you're ready to reenter the rattle and hum of life.

@

Schedule a little peace and quiet
into the busyness and noise of life.

Ask where the good way is, and walk in it,
and you will find rest for your souls.

JEREMIAH 6:16

Put your trust in God, my boys,
and keep your powder dry!

The Navigator

Six U.S. Army Special Forces soldiers were training near the Florida swamps. They were out on a hot, moonless night after three days of tough maneuvers. This night, they were to traverse a dense forest, carrying a metal raft, and then to navigate the swamps and capture an enemy camp. Deprived of sleep and nearly all sustenance for 32 hours, the men were exhausted. They marched four miles and finally reached the swamp. They quietly slid the boat into the water, boarded and began the tangled journey, relying only on a navigator's compass. He would whisper, "Left four degrees," "Hard right," and so on. They had slid on for awhile with no course adjustments. Suddenly, through the reeds, there appeared a sight that none of the men remembered from their map: It was an immense bridge—supporting a major highway. They were way off course; the navigator had fallen asleep.

It's comforting to know that in the often exhausting muck of life, we have a Navigator, a voice in the darkness whispering, if we listen, "This is the way; walk here." He never falters, never tires, and never sleeps.

@

We may feel in the dark, but we know we're always on course when we follow our Navigator.

Whether you turn to the right or to the left,
your ears will hear a voice behind you, saying,
"This is the way; walk in it."

ISAIAH 30:21

11

Possess your soul with patience.

The Waiting Game

When we travel by air, we must be open to the possibility of inconvenience, in particular, waiting. We could contend with late flights, cancelled flights, weather delays, and mechanical problems. Nearly every frequent flier has become well acquainted with each airport concourse, gift shop and grossly overpriced eatery because of a layover gone amok. Consider the person who has become one with his seat while stuck in a plane sanctioned to a runway for an indeterminate amount of time. Frustration erupts when we realize these situations are totally out of our control.

Yet, would we really want to fly into a snowstorm or risk a mechanically defunct plane? Isn't it better to suffer the wait than to be in a circumstance that could endanger our lives? The same holds true in our travels through life. So often, we have our eyes fixed on a particular destination, but our plans may seem thwarted. As we must trust the pilot, the mechanics and air traffic control when we fly, we must also trust the Chief Pilot as we make our way through life. God knows the whole picture, and if we seek His will, He will get us to the right destination in the way that is best for each one of us.

◉

When caught in a holding pattern,
we can trust that the Chief Pilot
will never steer us wrong.

Wait on the LORD: be of good courage,
and he shall strengthen thine heart:
wait, I say, on the LORD.

PSALM 27:14 KJV

Nothing will come of nothing. Dare mighty things.

Living Large

Attorney Ken Wills, a large, formidable man, sporting suspenders and cigar motioned the journalist to join him at the mahogany conference table.

"I understand you come from a family of dreamers and daredevils," the journalist began.

"Yes, my brothers were Wilbur and Orville Wright of hang gliding fame," Ken said with pride. "My brother Bobby holds a place in the *Guinness World Book of World Records,* and he's featured in the Smithsonian movie, *To Fly.* He's that little speck you see gliding among treacherous Hawaiian cliffs."

Ken continued, "Bobby soared to great heights personally as well. His contagious smile and incessant encouragement inspired all who knew him to reach for the stars and make their dreams come true. Bobby literally flew among eagles and was dubbed, 'an eagle among men.' He ascended into eternity doing what he loved most."

Ken handed the journalist a portion of a memoir written by his mother about Bobby:

Everything Bobby did was on an oversized scale. It seemed he would appear at any moment on a new contraption, a bigger and better hang glider, a taller bicycle . . . even now the memory of him looms large.

The journalist smiled pensively. "What a powerful legacy your brother has left—to live and love in larger-than-life proportions."

◎

Dare to dream—and make those dreams come true. Dare to help others do so, too.

I have come that they may have life, and have it to the full.

JOHN 10:10

I sought the simple life that nature yields.

God in the Details

A pastor was giving a sermon on the mundane details of life. In his fervor to drive home his point, he said, "You get up in the same old house, eat the same old thing, drive the same old route to the same old job, return to the same old wife . . . ." Realizing his error, the good reverend looked up to see one old-time parishioner, whose wife was known for being tirelessly difficult, nodding vigorously. The pastor had to avert his eyes from the parishioner, who could hardly control his chuckling through the rest of the sermon.

All of us would like, at times, to trade in the everyday aspects of our lives. Yet, all things, after time, become mundane. Brother Lawrence, a 17th century monk, suggested a fresh approach to life. His philosophy, also the title of the book containing his thoughts, is the practice of the presence of God. Brother Lawrence believed that we can sense God's presence while carrying out the daily routines of life—even contentedly peeling potatoes while communing with God.

We can "practice" looking, listening, and noticing as we go about the daily grind. There is beauty and opportunity for peace and thankfulness in the smallest elements of life.

⊙

One of the surest signs of a strong inner life is the ability to find meaning within the mundane.

Do not worry about your life, what you will eat or drink; or about your body, what you will wear. Is not life more important than food, and the body more important than clothes?

MATTHEW 6:25

17

To know even one life has breathed
easier because you lived . . .
this is to have succeeded.

Monkey Love

There stood the tall man in a business suit sporting a furry creature at his side. It was the new superintendent Dr. Sandy Outlar, walking the halls of Norfolk Christian Schools with a stuffed gorilla dangling down his torso. He was busy captivating the imaginations of the knee-high folks—introducing important ideas and lessons along with his tree-swingin' friend.

Dr. Outlar captured more than little hearts—in time he captured big hearts, too. As the first weeks of school rolled by, parents began to hear of the famous doctor and his sidekick through their children. The positive impact was obvious. Dr. Outlar had had an unhappy, difficult, and often dark childhood. But he purposed that he would do anything in his power—including forgetting his pride—in order to teach kids what's important, to brighten the day of even one child.

Many people have experienced extreme sadness, neglect, and disappointment in life. How wonderful it is when people can take disappointment, turn it into motivation, and show others the very kindness they went without. No doubt, the goodness comes back to them as well.

Good, when shared,
expands exponentially.

As God's chosen people . . . clothe yourselves
with compassion, kindness, humility . . .

COLOSSIANS 3:12

Trouble is as trouble is handled.

Inner Vision

Anyone who has seen pianist Ken Medema play knows that his brand of inspirational music reaches people on the level of heart and soul. His concerts are met with roaring applause and standing ovations. Aside from simply being a top-notch musician, Ken has a mission—to inspire people of all faiths, all walks of life, to worship God, and to bring people together through song. A "music therapist," Ken laments that people in our country don't gather and join voices around the piano as they used to. He believes that singing is a beautiful and positive expression, and he wishes to use his music and philosophy to help others.

Ken has also been blind from birth. Yet he doesn't consider it a detriment. At one concert in Manilla, Philippines, he expressed that he considered his lack of sight a blessing, that he would not wish his life any other way. Ken, through his attitude and sensitivity to the benefits of sound, has achieved an inner vision—a more excellent and powerful tool for effective living. When life's challenges meet us, we would do well to look beyond, to achieve inner vision to help us overcome and live above the difficulties of life.

@

God can give us the inner vision we
need to look beyond our circumstances.

"These things I have spoken to you, so that in Me you may have peace. In the world you have tribulation, but take courage; I have overcome the world."

JOHN 16:33 NASB

"I want to go home and be with <u>my</u> people."

Going Home

As teenagers, many of us couldn't wait to get out of the house, get out on our own—forge a life in newfound autonomy. Our society—and, in part, instinct—tells us this is the way it should be. This can be a great time of growth. Yet the longer we are away, the more we may realize that home isn't such a bad place to be. If we are willing to admit it, we may actually long to enter the familiar door, see the comforting sights, and take in the unforgettable scents that comprise our past.

There's nothing like the sense of ease and fulfillment we experience when we are in the presence of those who know and accept us. Some people may not have that kind of association with family; but there are friends whose very presence is like going home.

As we grow older, we often find it difficult to make time for the places and people we cherish. Like the little five-year-old who found school an alien place devoid of "his people," we look forward to being in the presence of "our people." Family, friends, and the familiar places they inhabit can be a shelter, a refreshing respite for mind, body, and spirit.

֎

Carve out time to spend with your people—whoever and wherever they may be.

It is right for me to feel this way about all of you, since I have you in my heart.

PHILIPPIANS 1:7

I shall love you in December
with the love given in May!

Seasons of Marriage

A sister, married two years, called her older brother, who had been married seven years. She was feeling glum, thinking about how her relationship with her husband had changed; there wasn't the same excitement as when they were newly married. A few days later, she received a letter from her wise and creative sibling. It read. . . .

Dear Sis:

Marriages go through seasons. Things can't always stay hot. Marriage is more like that favorite comfortable shirt you love to wear than a flashy evening dress. (But the evening dress does come out from time to time—and it's great when it does!) Ecclesiastes says, "There is a time and season for everything. . . ."

A time to weep. I'm not sure I understood what it meant to be "one" in marriage, until we went down a rough road together; one that had plenty of shared sorrow—and support and love for each other.

A time to laugh. Life and people are absurd. And the longer you live with someone, the more you see of the real person, and the more you experience together that's downright funny. Never underestimate the power of laughter to break up a good fight.

A time for war. Sometimes fights are good and need to be had to move beyond differences and reach understanding. We've had hot and cold wars!

A time for peace. There's nothing quite like the relief and joy when "all is calm and bright" between man and wife.

As someone who's known you all your life, I know you're not perfect, and neither is your man. But you are both wonderful human beings who are perfect for each other. Hang in! The best is yet to come.

Love, Your bro,

@

Relax with the seasons of marriage and watch
your love grow with the perspective that
only many years of shared
experiences can bring.

*Give thanks in all circumstances,
for this is God's will for you
in Christ Jesus.*

I Thessalonians 5:18

The great man is he who does
not lose his child's heart.

Elevate Yourself

A seasoned businessman attending a convention in Atlanta was eager to unwind at his hotel on the last evening of his stay. Visions of salmon and she-crab soup were swimming in his head, and the pressures of the week would soon be put to bed.

Mind and body weary from the steady pace of speakers and meetings; he leaned his tall frame against the clear, glass back of the elevator. A mother and a blonde girl who was all smiles boarded the elevator. The businessman and the mother exchanged polite nods.

In the instant the elevator lurched upward, the girl squealed with delight, "WOW!" as she held on tight to the brass railing, overcome by the miraculous ascent.

The man shook his head in surprise as if he'd just been awakened by a bucket of cold water. He laughed at both himself and the silly girl. The girl's mother smiled sheepishly and said, "Her father works for an elevator company. You'd think this would get old after a while."

As the man exited the elevator, he thought to himself, *If I could interject even a tenth of that childlike enthusiasm into my days, what an exciting, elevating ride my life and work could be!*

/⊚

We can often learn how to incorporate
God-given joy into our lives,
by observing the wonder of children.

From the lips of children and infants
you have ordained praise.

PSALM 8:2

Little deeds of kindness, little words of love,
Help to make earth happy like the heaven above.

 # Thinking of You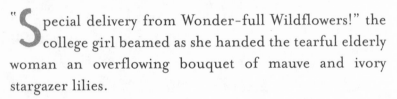

"Special delivery from Wonder-full Wildflowers!" the college girl beamed as she handed the tearful elderly woman an overflowing bouquet of mauve and ivory stargazer lilies.

"Happy Birthday!" she announced later, as she bestowed the startled secretary with a crystal vase of long-stemmed yellow sunflowers.

"Congratulations!" she smiled, presenting the weary new mother with a porcelain stork filled with coral roses and baby's breath.

The flower girl nearly skipped back to the van after each delivery and thought, *I have the best job on the face of the planet. Everyone is always happy to see me!*

Yet she knew that the real reason people were happy to see her was that she was the gift-bearer for friends, family members, and lovers. These caring people knew the importance of reaching out to those they love during difficult times or special occasions, and letting their love be known. Flowers, a favorite candy or tea, or simply a card . . . a little gift can let people know not only that you value them, but that you've noticed something significant about them.

A little gift, thoughtfully chosen, can make a big impact.

The administration of this service not only supplieth the want of the saints, but is abundant also by many thanksgivings unto God.
II CORINTHIANS 9:12 KJV

Life is half spent before we know what it is.

Chip Off the Ol' Block

A young boy was outside on a warm summer's day, swinging his kid-sized golf club to hit his little plastic golf ball. His mom was looking out on this idyllic scene . . . her golden-haired son trying to imitate his dad. Her reverie was abruptly broken when she heard a string of expletives following a missed attempt at hitting the ball. She nearly flew to the backyard. "What did you say?" she said to her son. Trying to disguise his misdeed, he mumbled syllables that sounded similar. "I don't think so," said the mom. She marched her son to the front of the house, where her husband was working. "Would you like to know what your son just said?" She asked her son to repeat exactly what he had said. He repeated it, verbatim. The dad turned red. He was reminded, like a club over the head, that this was *his* standard response when *he* missed the ball. The father's penchant for golf wasn't the only thing this son had picked up from his dad.

It is always wise to watch what we say around children—but we grown-ups also are impressionable. What we put into our minds, what we see and hear, has a lot to do with what shapes our thinking and our speech.

@

Garbage in, garbage out
(and possibly even flung back to you!).

Be very careful, then, how you live—
not as unwise but as wise.

EPHESIANS 5:15

God hath His small interpreters;
The child must teach the man.

Summer Shelter

Young Jason's parents had recently divorced. His father was an oil company executive, and his mother was a painter who traveled extensively, so they arranged for Jason to spend the summer with his aunt on her ranch in the Texas country.

Rolling hills were alive with the reds and blues of Indian paintbrushes and bluebonnets. "Jason!" Aunt Ann greeted him with a warm hug. "Welcome—we're so happy to have you here!"

In spite of his hurt and confusion, Jason felt secure as his aunt and he walked around their ranch. Two golden retrievers joined them—followed by fuzzy little puppies. She showed him a tree house perched in the towering, twisted branches of a century-old oak. The shining lake promised early mornings and evenings of fishing with his uncle in their old sturdy boat. Ann and her husband had decided that they would do everything in their power to give Jason the freedom, support and fun that he so needed in his little life.

Many children, right in our own neighborhoods and families, don't experience the freedom of simply being a kid due to painful situations. A perfect, pain-free childhood isn't realistic; but we adults can help restore the joy and security that should accompany this time of life.

Provide a haven for children who need some of the security and pleasure of childhood returned.

[Jesus] said to them, "Whoever welcomes one of these little children in my name welcomes me."

MARK 9:36, 37

It is never too late to give up our prejudices.

The Test

One day, the pastor of a church in an affluent big city suburb decided he would try something. He wanted to take the pulse of the heart of his church. He grew out his whiskers. He went out and picked up a light, oversized jacket. He threw on a tattered large-brimmed cap, some old ripped work pants, dark sunglasses and a few smudges of "dirt." He looked like he'd been on the streets for weeks, and that was exactly what he wanted. He lingered, crouched down outside the church door as his parishioners entered, in their Sunday best, on a bitter-cold day. No one even so much as nodded at the street person.

The doors closed. It was time for church, but there was no sign of the pastor. After a few minutes, heads turned as the back doors swung open, and the filthy looking bum walked up the aisle and behind the pulpit. Before anyone could remove the intruder, the bum removed his hat and glasses and began to speak. A hush fell over the people as the pastor prayed and began, out of the normal sequence, to give the most unforgettable sermon this congregation had ever heard. The topic: "If you do it unto the least of these, you do it unto me."

We should take care not to become so wrapped up in going to God's house, that we forget to actually serve Him.

If ye fulfil the royal law according to the scripture, Thou shalt love thy neighbour as thyself, ye do well.

JAMES 2:8 KJV

Give a little love to a child, and
you get a great deal back.

A Lunch that Lasts

The advertising sales rep didn't have time to go to the school. He was working on a big account and was going to have to work late as it was. His wife had to attend a last-minute mandatory meeting over lunch, so here he was.

He stepped through the door, followed the brightly decorated corridor, and walked into the classroom. Knee-high tables were adorned with little paper cups brimming with the leaves of sprouting pinto beans. Finger-painted handprints graced homemade place mats, and peanut butter sandwiches were cut into butterfly shapes. He didn't have to look long for his daughter, who greeted him with an enthusiastic, "Daddy!"

Immediately, his demeanor and attitude changed. He was even disappointed to learn that several parents had been unable to attend. Consequently, he was bombarded with repeated requests of "Look at mine!" as children

searched for approval of their glittered egg carton cater-
pillar. What more appetizing lunch could be found?

The "ad dad" practically floated back to his car. He had
been treated like a celebrity and all he had done was spend
an hour with his daughter and her Lilliputian counter-
parts. He carried the elevated mood with him through the
rest of his day—and the lesson, the rest of his life.

@

When the pressing things of life drown
out the important things in life,
we should pause and re-prioritize.

*"Let the little children come to me, and
do not hinder them, for the kingdom
of heaven belongs to such as these."*

MATTHEW 19:14

Enter these enchanted woods, you who dare.

Rose Garden

It was perfect. Jim and Shirley Ruppert had all the right stuff: business savvy, gregarious personalities, and a penchant for gourmet cooking. Theirs would be one of the best bed and breakfast establishments in Nashville. They would call it "The Rose Garden" and display their award-winning collection of sweet smelling bushes in hues of peachy corals and candy apple reds.

Well-meaning friends warned of the risks of pouring thousands of dollars into renovating their basement into a guest suite. "Think about the headaches of dealing with the public," advised others.

There were days, especially in the beginning, when the Rupperts wondered if they were indeed crazy: *Would their American dream turn into a nightmare?* Time would tell, but neither of them wanted to look back and think, "What if?" So they followed their hearts and carefully plotted the course of their dream.

Years later, the profit-turning proprietors welcomed the legendary actor, Robert Duvall, to The Rose Garden Bed and Breakfast during the filming of *The Apostle*. You should have seen their nay-saying friends drop their jaws.

⊚

Does your heart house the stuff that dreams are made of? Remember that risks and dreams are the bricks and mortar of a life lived to the fullest.

Lord, all my desire is before You;
And my sighing is not hidden from You.
PSALM 38:9 NASB

O welcome pure-eyed Faith, white-handed Hope,
Thou hovering angel, girt with golden wings.

The Act of Faith

A couple had been trying to have a child for a number of years. They had pursued the medical route—at high cost and little success. Many people in their lives speculated as to the reasons for their lack of success in the baby department, comments ranging from the insensitive to the absurd. Yet through the disappointment, the couple strove to live according to what they believed: that God loves them, that He wants the best for them, and that God's best did not include, at that time, a biological child. They later came to experience the great joy of adopting a beautiful baby, one they believe was chosen specifically for them.

In *The Obedience of a Christian Man* William Tyndale says, "Let us arm our souls with the promises both of help *and* assistance." Belief in the promises even when the emotions tend to despair constitutes an important Christian skill. Faith should not, need not, change based on our varying emotions and desires. While "hope deferred" is difficult, we can find comfort in the fact that this stable Supreme Being is greater than our hearts, greater than well-meaning friends—and that He knows everything.

@

Faith is the oxygen in our spiritual journeys.

God is greater than our hearts, and he knows everything.

1 JOHN 3:20

God's mouth knows not to utter falsehood,
but he will perform each word.

The Frantic Fly Factor

Why is it when we're faced with uncertainty in a situation, we do everything but consult God? We read magazines and books, talk to friends, and get ourselves so tied up in mental knots that leave us confused and paralyzed. We are like frantic flies buzzing around in the circle of a lampshade, making many random moves, but getting nowhere fast.

Certainly, researching a matter can be good—even essential. And friends can be helpful in helping us sort out our thoughts—medical studies have shown us that the stress associated with people who bottle up their emotions can lead to great physical harm. Yet we must also check the frantic fly factor when we are in a difficult situation. Instead of bouncing from source to source, getting ourselves into a dither, we would do well to remember that God is watching and waiting for us to "chill out," get our thoughts focused, and go to Him with our concerns. Not only that, but we can do so with boldness, because we are His children. When we do so, in His time He will guide us from the lampshade to the open air of freedom.

Prior to flying all around creation, why not consult the Creator?

Let us therefore come boldly unto the throne
of grace, that we may obtain mercy,
and find grace to help in time of need.

HEBREWS 4:16 KJV

To do him any wrong was to beget
A kindness from him, for his heart was rich.

What Comes Around. . . .

A respected Army Staff Sergeant was in charge of new recruits at Ft. Bragg, North Carolina. As is typical, this man in charge gave the new "boys" a hard time. One new recruit was an eager young man named Gooding. It was Gooding's first day and the Staff Sergeant, asked him, "Gooding, does your hand fit a mop?" Gooding looked at his hand and said, "Yes, sir." The Staff Sergeant then suggested getting the latrine. This became a standard, and good-natured, exchange between the two men. The Staff Sergeant left the military for just over two years. If he wanted to reenter the Army, he would lose all previous rank.

The former Staff Sergeant re-enlisted, and came back in as a private. He got to the base and there, to his surprise, was Buck Sergeant Gooding. What's the first thing Gooding said? "Hey, private, does your hand fit a mop?" The exchange was friendly, and the re-enlisted private soon climbed the ranks to surpass his former title. Yet he learned what all of us should keep in mind: It is important at all times, in all professions, to treat subordinates—or anyone—with the kindness and respect everyone deserves.

Make sure what you give is what
you'd like to come back to you.

A kind man benefits himself.

PROVERBS 11:17

A perfect faith would lift us
absolutely above fear.

Facing the Future

We humans have a fascination with the future. Look in the back of any popular culture magazine. You will see ads with cosmic symbols and women in jeweled turbans claiming, "Answers by Real Psychics" or "Turn Today's Doubt Into Tomorrow's Success." Horoscopes, TV, and radio psychics—everywhere we turn, people claim to know the unknown secrets of tomorrow.

Much of this need to know comes from fear. Humans are limited to knowledge of past and present. Yet we aren't without hope. In the Bible, Jesus promises that we can look at the future without fear because our hope is in Him. We can find great peace in this promise. Still, tomorrow is a mystery.

Perhaps our chief goal in this life should be to focus all our energy on the present. As the writer George MacDonald recommends, we can trust God with the future. We can let it unfold as a gift from Him. And what an exciting way to approach the future . . . as a grand mystery, waiting to unfold and, most importantly, orchestrated by the One who not only "makes the storm clouds," but Who knows and loves us intimately.

@

Yesterday, history.
Tomorrow, a mystery.
Today, a gift—
that's why it's the present.

Ask the LORD for rain in the springtime;
it is the LORD who makes the storm clouds.
He gives showers of rain to men . . .
diviners see visions that lie; they tell dreams
that are false, they give comfort in vain.

ZECHARIAH 10:1-2

Very little is needed to make a happy life.

Now What?

A married couple had spent months planning every detail of their dream home—a gabled roof, a sprawling porch, and brass fixtures in every bathroom. These were the rewards of years of meticulous saving and planning. After they moved in there was so much to do. The wife spent hours on end shopping for couches, curtains, paintings, and floral arrangements to display the beauty of their home. It was exciting and exhausting, but always rewarding when at day's end when they would sit and admire the masterpiece of each room. Once the last room was painted, molding up and décor complete, they began to feel a strange sense of discontent settling over them. The fulfillment of their dream, while exactly as they had planned, wasn't enough. The operative phrase: "Now what?"

So often in life we believe, whether consciously or unconsciously, that if we could just get that car, that house, that new kitchen—whatever we desire—that we would achieve a completion that will bring happiness. None of these things is wrong—on the contrary, God wants us to enjoy "the fruits of our labor." But we are mistaken when we believe anything but our personal relationships, foremost our relationship with God, will bring true contentment.

Enjoy possessions—
live for people.

Set your minds on things above,
not on earthly things.

COLOSSIANS 3:2

A feeling of sadness and longing
That is not akin to pain,
And resembles sorrow only
As the mist resembles the rain.

Inevitable Grief

Chilean writer Isabel Allende was interviewed on National Public Radio. She spoke of her daughter, Paula, who contracted a disease, porphyria, that took her life . . . she, a beautiful young girl on the cusp of a bright future. Naturally, Allende experienced immeasurable grief, a pain which may never fully disappear. Yet Allende made a curious and powerful statement—that grief, sadness and pain are just as much a part of this life as love, joy and health, that we must expect and even, in a sense, embrace the sadness and disappointment.

Loss through death is one of the hardest things in life, yet there are other things in our lives that create a sense of despair: loss of health, a broken relationship, changes in the seasons of life, unmet expectations. Christ himself said, "In this world you will have trouble, but take heart, for I have overcome the world" (John 16:33 NIV). We need not be surprised when the painful situations emerge—and we shouldn't be afraid of the feelings that come from these situations. We can ask God to help us keep our heads up when faced with the cold winds of disappointment, and He will grant us the strength and peace to make it through the winter into a better spring. That's a promise.

@

The "man of sorrows" will help us bear our grief.

In the same way, the Spirit helps us in our weakness.
We do not know what we ought to pray for, but the Spirit himself
intercedes for us with groans that words cannot express.

ROMANS 8:26

The most astonishing thing about
miracles is that they happen.

The Man in the Tree

A woman headed home after a day of teaching and picked up her four-year-old. She strapped her tyke into his car seat and drove off in her small car. Heading into the driveway, she put the car in park and got out to check the mail. In a matter of seconds, she saw the car rolling forward down the sloped driveway and over a thirty-foot embankment—her little one still in the back seat. The mother's heart raced wildly as she ran after the car. It finally came to rest upside down among a dense pile of leaves, but the top was completely smashed. She called to her son frantically as she struggled to open the door.

There, to her relief, was a bewildered but perfectly fine little boy. She grabbed him, sobbing. "Thank you, God," she repeated repeatedly. Later, as mother tucked son into bed, she asked, "Honey, weren't you scared?" He answered matter-of-factly, "No, because that man in the tree caught me."

Though we can't see them, heavenly beings are with us, watching over us. We would do well to thank God for His protection—we may not even be aware of the many "near misses" we've had in a day.

🌀

God is here and so are His angels,
even though we can't see them
with human eyes, we can feel
them with human hearts.

He will give His angels charge concerning you,
To guard you in all your ways.

PSALM 91:11 NASB

53

One God, one law, one element,
And one far-off divine event
To which the whole creation moves.

To Know and Be Known

It may be a sibling, a spouse, or a long-time friend, but most of us have someone in our lives who seems to click with our thought patterns. A shared laugh, a knowing wink or a look of understanding—being with this person is rejuvenating. This person is a kindred spirit and one of life's great gifts. Yet this individual, however perceptive, cannot know us fully. In fact, no one—not this person, our spouse, our childhood friends, and our own parents—can know us in any comprehensive way. And while we find great pleasure in knowing and discovering more about people in our lives, we will never know anyone fully either. Sometimes it seems we don't even know ourselves.

We certainly don't know the limitless mind of God, but He does know and understand us on a level deeper than any human kindred spirit can, more than we know ourselves. When we ask Him for direction, He not only knows what we're saying, but what we *really* mean, where we're coming from, where we're headed—and where we should be headed. We can talk to God often and with absolute frankness, knowing that He always connects with us.

When we talk to the Creator,
we will always be met
with understanding.

There is not a word in my tongue, but, lo,
O Lord, thou knowest it altogether.

PSALM 139:4 KJV

The unexamined life is not worth living.

Reality-Based Living

Carol Burnett devotees might well remember her spoof of the washed up film star who wouldn't let go of the past. We may have laughed at the portrayal (and it was funny). Yet when we consider the reality of this person, we can see the sadness of the situation. This woman had nothing but her stardom on which to base her identity. When well past her "glamour prime," she continued to wear party gowns and to cover her wrinkled face with heavy burlesque-style make-up. She would stumble about in too-high heels asking, "Do you remember me?"

In our media-drenched, youth and glamour-oriented culture, we are told that looking good physically and appearing successful to others is paramount. And who doesn't desire these things? Yet when those desires become our overriding motivators in life, we are choosing a life that is devoid of substance. We are robbing ourselves of reality and others of the opportunity to really know us. When we base our identity on who we are, unique individuals made in the image of God and loved by God, we have something solid to build on. This is where we can find true and lasting richness—a confidence and fullness we can carry with us through all the seasons of life.

🌀

Live authentically.

*Through the grace given to me I say to
every man among you not to think more
highly of himself than he ought to think;
but to think so as to have sound judgment,
as God has allotted to each a measure of faith.*

ROMANS 12:3 NASB

Pay attention to matters of importance.

The Obvious Question

Two sharp editors of a popular music magazine would often exchange files electronically. It was customary for them to write notes to one another within the text of an article, in big, bold capital letters. It was around the holidays, and the January issue was running behind. Articles had come in late. Staff had been out sick. And now it was up to the editors to make the print deadline. One of the smaller articles was about a respected, but not very well-known, singer/songwriter. The senior editor flew through the articles and sent them on to the junior editor. He, in turn, breezed through, getting the magazine ready to go into production, and then to print. The issue barely made it to press, and because of the tight schedule, they didn't see a proof before the final printing. The issue arrived. They flipped through, and Tom, the junior editor, nearly sank to his knees as he saw, in the center of the singer/songwriter article, in big, bold capital letters: TOM: IS THIS GUY DEAD? That day, the magazine received a telephone call. It was the singer/songwriter. "You can let Tom know," he said, "that I am not yet deceased."

In our work and personal lives, it is important not to let circumstances blind us to what is most important to see.

@

We often miss the obvious in front of us when our thoughts are far ahead of us.

You are looking at things as they are outwardly.

2 CORINTHIANS 10:7 NASB

59

No man's knowledge here can
go beyond his experience.

Circles

Have you ever noticed that following God's lead rarely takes you in a straight line? More often, the trail that leads to where God wants us winds in zigzags and circles. We can find ourselves scratching our heads and asking, "Lord, what was *that* all about?"

We've grown up hearing the adage, "The shortest distance between two points is a straight line," but in God's book, there seems to be value in detours.

Maybe it has to do with matters of the heart. It may be that in God's eyes, growing our hearts, healing our hearts, and preparing our hearts for a particular destination is just as important as arriving.

This is often true of career and family moves. We want to think that a particular job or a specific town is where we will stay for a good while—maybe even forever. However, we need to be open to the concept that sometimes God leads us to a job or a town for a season. It would help to pray, "God, give me the grace to trust that Your path is accomplishing Your will in me. And help me not to obsess about the destination."

When it seems like the path of
your life has you running around
in circles, remember that God
may be busy preparing your heart
to handle a particular destination.

*Those who live in accordance with
the Spirit have their minds set on
what the Spirit desires.*

ROMANS 8:5

How good is man's life, the mere living!
How fit to employ All the heart and
the soul and the senses forever in joy!

Chief Grandma

A 70-year-old, recently widowed woman bought a house in a new town. This woman loved to travel, and when she was ready to hit the road again, she stopped by the fire station a block from her house. She introduced herself and asked if the firefighters would drive by and check on her house occasionally while she was away. They did and she, in turn, began to bake for them. After time, she would stay for coffee and join in the lively firehouse banter. As firemen would move to other stations, they'd say, "Grandma, don't forget about me!" So she began visiting other stations. In time, she baked and delivered to every station—124 shifts in all.

At age 91, though she can no longer drive, "Chief Grandma" continues to bake. Firefighters take her to stations on their days off. They all know and love Grandma, who is perennially upbeat. She says that when she first drove into town, she made a conscious choice. Instead of sitting in her house, feeling sorry for herself, she decided to get out and to do for others. It made all the difference for her. For any of us, at any age, making that choice will make all the difference in our lives, too.

@

We are never too old, or
too young, to make the choice
to get out and live life.

*I have come that they may have life
and have it to the full.*

JOHN 10:10

The God who gave us life gave us
liberty at the same time.

There for the Taking

While no human can rightfully claim to have "created" his or her children, kids can be likened to beings fashioned, in a manner of speaking, in a parent's image or likeness. In this relationship, the parent most often experiences a sense of profound love for this little one. This love translates into protectiveness and a desire to provide a secure environment, but also one in which a child can grow and progress. As they grow, however, children normally strike out on their own, forging their independence. This forging happens with varying degrees of consequence. If only wise parents could orchestrate their children's steps, save them from mistakes—If only children would ask for their advice.

We are in much the same boat in our relationship to our heavenly Father. God, in His great love, has the same desire for us, his children—to grow and develop—but to do so in His will, with His guidance. Yet parents are

human, with all the limitations that come with this desig-
nation. And God? Well, He is infinite in wisdom, knowledge, power, and understanding. And He so wants the
best for us—if only His children would ask.

✿

No one needs travel through life
without God's wisdom and guidance.

The LORD giveth wisdom: out of his mouth
cometh knowledge and understanding.

PROVERBS 2:6 KJV

65

See how these Christians love one another.

Living Masterpieces

A be Lincoln said that friendship could well be one of nature's greatest masterpieces. When we really think about a masterpiece, like Michelangelo's work on the ceiling of the Sistine Chapel, we realize that creating something of great artistic merit requires immense effort and time. The more exquisite the work, the greater effort and time. It took Michelangelo four grueling years, between 1508 and 1512, to complete the work on the ceiling of the Sistine Chapel—over 300 figures in amazing and overwhelming detail. His effort during that time was so intense that his vision and very appearance became altered—he aged five years for every one he gave to his work.

A healthy friendship is an open canvas, one that deserves our best effort. We all have creative power when it comes to our relationships—we can brush over them quickly, creating a less-than-pleasing, surface piece of art, or we can devote the time, thought and energy that, over time, will take the shape of an intricate and beautiful work of art.

When time and energy are devoted
to a friendship in great measure,
it becomes a living work of art.

Now about brotherly love we do not need
to write you, for you yourselves have been
taught by God to love each other . . . yet we
urge you, brothers, to do so more and more.

I THESSALONIANS 4:9-10

Over all, rocks, wood, and water, brooded
the spirit of repose, and the silent energy of
nature stirred the soul to its inmost depths.

Creation Calls

It is a clear, cloudless night, out where the city lights don't interfere. You look up into the black of the heavens at a myriad of stars—some millions of dim lights clustered together. Waves of stars that make up the Milky Way Galaxy, singular bright stars, maybe planets. The vastness is overwhelming. You sit in the quiet of a summer night, and one star soars and plummets out of the sky. You marvel at this common, yet glorious, spectacle.

The endless sky, a towering mountain, and the tiniest delicate flower—all display the immense power and grandeur of God. One would think that the sheer vastness of nature would overwhelm or put one in a state of unease. Yet the opposite is true: something about spending time in the quiet of God's magnificent creation seems to do good for our souls, to set us aright. Perhaps it's because God is revealed through His creation. We also learn in Scripture that nature was created largely for our pleasure, and while it is no longer pristine, it still resonates in our very beings. Whether it's catching a sunrise one morning or getting away to the mountains or the sea, make certain to allow the beauty of nature to rejuvenate your soul.

⟨◎⟩

The soul hears the voice of God speaking through his natural creation.

He makes me lie down in green pastures,
he leads me beside quiet waters,
he restores my soul.

PSALM 23:2-3

Don't confuse constant activity
with a meaningful life.

 Stop the Madness

The buzzword today is "busy." Many parents these days say they feel like chauffeurs, running their children from one sports practice to another. There is play group, dance class, and birthday parties. People find themselves constantly racing between activities—working long hours, getting gifts for the next occasion, going to dinner parties, or any manner of party wherein someone is selling the longest-burning candle or the best kitchen gadgets for the new millennium. The pace can become dizzying; yet we still attempt to cram everything we can into our schedules.

We as a culture are so future- and production-oriented, we can hardly stand to leave our date books unscheduled. We want to make certain we have it all planned out—nothing left to chance. What if we miss something? In matters of finance and time management, this is wise. But have we so scheduled our kids that they have no room for creativity—or for simply being kids? Are we so jammed up with activity that we constantly feel exhausted and behind the game? Could it be that we are controlled by our date books and not leaving room for the spontaneous working of God in our lives? Chilling out at home? Not buying anything for, say, a week? That's perfectly okay.

Don't live so much in a whirlwind
of activity that when you look back,
all you see is an unidentifiable blur.

He who guards his way guards his life.

PROVERBS 16:17

71

And the tear that is wiped with a little address,
May be follow'd perhaps by a smile.

Venus and Mars in the Car

A young man and woman had been dating for about six months. The man picked her up for a date just after work, after a bad day complete with a conflict with a supervisor. As they drove, she began to tell him about her day. The well-meaning man instantly told her what she might have done to prevent the situation. The woman snapped, "I don't want you to fix the problem, I want you to sympathize with me, put your hand on my shoulder." "Hmm," he thought about it. About a week later, they were late to a wedding rehearsal. The woman was driving. She said to the man, the navigator, "Where do I turn?" He paused, put his hand on her shoulder and said, "Oh, don't you hate when you don't know where to turn. That's so frustrating." You can guess where the conversation went from there.

While his timing and motive may be in question, the young man got the message. (The next wedding they attended was theirs!) In relationships, it is important to let other people know what you expect from them—and to learn what other people expect of you. People aren't mind readers, and we can store up loads of frustration and bitterness believing they should be.

◎

When you want to achieve a heartfelt goal, remember to aim beyond the target, realizing that extra time and extra effort may produce extra-ordinary results.

To sum up, let all be harmonious, sympathetic, brotherly, kindhearted, and humble in spirit.

1 PETER 3:8 NASB

I know only that what is moral is
what you feel good after and what is
immoral is what you feel bad after.

Standing Up

Movies like *The Fugitive* or *The Shawshank Redemption* tell the story of a person who's been wrongly accused. Our hearts pound as they plot and plan escape from wrongful imprisonment and work to clear their names. We are gripped with righteous indignation at their ill treatment. After all, there they were, model citizens doing the right thing, and look what happened. They don't deserve punishment, and we cheer for them right through to the end.

Why, in real life, especially in the business world, are we so hesitant to stand up for what is right? Maybe it's obvious: In a movie, we can cheer and support the "good guy" without consequences. In the real world, of course, everything comes with consequences, and standing up for what's right doesn't always make us look good. Hey, look what happened to John the Baptist when he called Herod on his immoral behavior. (He was beheaded.) No one likes a person who makes waves, right? Perhaps when we come upon a situation that seems to demand a moral voice, we should think less of how we'll "come off" and more of how we'll feel inside—and how God looks at our inaction—if we don't do what's right.

◎

Remember, right makes might—ultimately.

*Our light and momentary troubles
are achieving for us an eternal glory
that far outweighs them all.*

II CORINTHIANS 4:17

Careless words become burning arrows
that pierce the very hearts of men.

 # Searing Words

Seven-year-old Marta began to cook dinner for her family of four. It was the early 1900s. Her mother had become ill, and Marta was the natural choice. She had a younger sister, Gracey, who wasn't fond of domestic tasks. She would rather read or do puzzles. Gracey's parents believed her to be intelligent and weren't stern with her regarding her chores. Marta, being very adept at the household tasks, carried the weight. Marta was creative, a good artist—and she was also very bright. When it came time for the girls, who were close in age, to go to college, their parents saw fit for Gracey to attend, but not Marta. She was heartbroken. Her father said to her, "Well, you're not as smart as Grace. But don't worry, you're a good cook."

Marta is now 90. She has lived a full and exciting life. She's an avid reader and has an amazing mind. Eighty years later, she still talks about those words from her father. She still believes she's not very smart. The words we use have great power. We must take care to use that power for good, especially when we are talking about the characteristics or abilities of another person.

@

Words have great power for ill or good—measure and use your words with care.

Let your speech be always with grace, seasoned with salt.

COLOSSIANS 4:6 KJV

God moves in a mysterious way,
His wonders to perform . . .
Deep in unfathomable mines
Of never-failing skill,
He treasures up his bright designs,
And works his sov'reign will.

Train of Woes

Why is it that the bad things in life seem to gang up on us? It can be small annoyances: the alarm doesn't go off, coffee spills on you in the worst place at the worst time, a car won't start. It can be major ones, like dealing with serious illness, financial loss, or death. When a train of negative events or circumstances pulls into our station, we often take it personally. We ask, "Why me?"

The poet William Cowper in *Light Shining out of Darkness* wrote:

Ye fearful saints, fresh courage take,
The clouds ye so much dread
Are big with mercy, and shall break
In blessings on your head.

So too with us. When we're faced with the annoyances or the traumas of life, we need not waste energy trying to place blame or take them personally, as if God is singling us out. What we can do is turn to Him and ask for the peace of mind and strength to rise above.

When the train of woes pulls into your station, climb aboard—just be sure to talk with the Conductor.

We do not have a high priest who is unable
to sympathize with our weaknesses . . .
Let us then approach the throne of grace
with confidence, so that we may receive
mercy and find grace to help us in our
time of need.

HEBREWS 4:15-16

I could never divide myself from any
man upon the difference of an opinion,
or be angry with his judgment
for not agreeing with me.

Agreeing to Disagree

The Connelly family numbered fifteen, with thirteen kids and two parents. On Sundays, the family would gather in the tiny kitchen of their home, along with spouses and their children and family friends, eat ham and potatoes, and talk. There was but one bathroom for up to 30 people, always with a line trailing up the stairs. Visitors were amazed, sitting or leaning as best possible on a remaining bit of counter space, at the conversation. The Connellys would bring up all the "taboo" subjects: current issues, politics, and even religion. They would discuss and even launch into red-faced arguing. Visitors might feel uncomfortable or become worried until the Connellys would diffuse the discussion with laughter—a lot of it. And when the evening would come to its close, the Connellys would spend an hour saying good night, making sure to kiss and hug everyone present.

We all have different opinions on at least one subject with the people in our lives. It is okay to discuss, to express our point of view. But we mustn't sacrifice important relationships due to difference of opinion on issues that, in the end, don't influence the most important aspects of our lives.

/◎

After a friendly family fight,
be sure to hug and kiss good night.

Be completely humble and gentle; be patient,
bearing with one another in love.

Ephesians 4:2

To me every hour of the light and dark is a miracle,
Every cubic inch of space is a miracle.

Half Full or Half Empty?

Recent studies performed by UCLA and the Mayo Clinic revealed that optimists are not only happier, but they are healthier. They get sick less frequently. They recover more quickly from surgery and injury. We've all met people who immediately consider the worst case scenario—maybe we fall into this category. Pessimism, if not checked, can become pathological. It's destructive to the negative thinker—and it can rob innocent bystanders of their joy. Pessimists feel as if nothing will go well for them. They may want to protect themselves from disappointment, just in case things don't live up to expectations (and they probably won't).

God, through Scripture, gives us so many reasons to have hope. He loves us unconditionally. He promises to guide and comfort us when we seek Him. He guarantees to give us wisdom when we but ask. Those are big-picture ideas. But how do we get from "half empty" to "half full?" Start by noticing and being thankful for the small things: your health, the fact that you have food, live in a warm house, can get a good cup of Java on nearly every street corner. Practice taking that same thankful attitude to larger situations and work at steering clear of negativity. You will be happier, healthier—and you may even live longer.

⊚

One who recognizes the everyday
"miracles" of life can't help
but live with a hopeful heart.

I will hope continually, and will
yet praise thee more and more.

PSALM 71:14 KJV

You catch more flies with honey
than with vinegar.

Wise Compromise

A mother faced a difficult situation. Her seventeen-year-old, college-bound daughter was dating a local boy, and the two wanted to be married—right away. The mother had a strong sense that this was not the right match for either of them. Her daughter had a genius IQ and her mother wanted her to have the opportunity to use her wonderful mind and believed she would thrive in the university environment. The young man, a year her senior, was a fine boy, but he didn't have the aspirations or drive that the mother would like to have seen. This mother could easily have flown off the handle and said "absolutely not." Instead, this wise woman said, "Okay, you can be married—after my daughter attends one semester of college." True to this mother's instincts, her daughter thrived in school and discovered that campus life had a lot to offer in the way of young collegiate men. She broke off her engagement before she even returned home for the holiday break.

So often, especially when we are faced with situations that could carry long-term consequences, we are quick to lower the boom by brashly speaking our mind. What is better, and more effective most every time, is evaluating and presenting our thoughts with wisdom and tact.

◉

Run all words through the filter of wisdom before letting them hit the air.

A man of knowledge uses words with restraint.

PROVERBS 17:27

If we had no winter, the spring
would not be so pleasant: if we did
not sometimes taste of adversity,
prosperity would not be so welcome.

Weathering the Seasons

Seventeenth-century writer Anne Bradstreet was no stranger to "winter" and "adversity." Born and bred on an upper-class English estate, her life in England would most likely have been one of ease. Instead, after marrying Simon Bradstreet, their Puritan beliefs led them to journey to New England. Life in the colony was harsh, with poverty, illness, and extreme climates. What is more, women who were educated, who read and wrote, were considered ungodly.

Anne, faithful to her religion, spoke out against this attitude in her writing, discreetly, but she made no great public declaration. Her work was not published until after her death. Through everything, she held fast to her faith. Her view of life could be summed up in the poem, "Upon the Burning of Our House." She laments the loss of the place "Where oft I sat and long did lie: /here stood that trunk and there that chest. . . . " Then she says, "Raise up thy thoughts above the sky/ . . .Thou hast an house on high erect/Framed by that mighty Architect/With glory richly furnished." This strong mother of eight wrestled with life, challenged the norms, but sought to become stronger, to fight against her own will to gain a heavenly perspective of life.

/◎

Behind the harsh winds of winter comes the gentle breeze of spring.

Perseverance must finish its work so that
you may be mature and complete,
not lacking anything.

JAMES 1:4

Most of the luxuries, and many of the so-called comforts of life are not only not indispensable, but positive hindrances to the elevation of mankind.

Striving to Simplify

In today's American society, clutter has become such a great problem that there is an actual movement, a focused trend, toward simplicity. Now, people are making their living as clutter consultants, helping other people to de-clutter—and stay that way. Yet, when it comes to hurling our possessions into the river, we are fighting upstream. We are bombarded with advertising and TV and movie images that show people with better stuff—more compact, more hip, more . . . money. Are we really living if we're not visiting one of the hottest trend restaurants at least once a week? The more we have, the more we want (and at the same time, don't want, packing out our homes and our psyches). We are so programmed to buy—even if it's a latte at the local coffee shop. This love-hate relationship with possessions creates a chaos that can keep us from truly enjoying life.

If your clutter, or your craving for more stuff, is taking over, simplify! Give away what you don't need or use. Enjoy the space in your home (and in your head). Try not buying anything aside from the basics for a week. Make it two. Re-program your thinking by finding simple pleasures that you can enjoy without dropping coin.

⊚

Give yourself some open space.

Do not store up for yourselves treasures on earth. . . . for where your treasure is, there your heart will be also.

MATTHEW 6:19, 21

89

To a close-shorn sheep,
God gives wind by measure.

Faith Mode

God knows everything. We say this. We believe it. But living as if we are certain this is true is no easy task. Samuel Taylor Coleridge, the poet and theologian wrote, "Faith is an affirmation and an act/that bids eternal truth be fact." He understood the battle between what we feel and what we know to be eternally true.

Our changing moods are possibly one of the most difficult obstacles we have to overcome in maturing and growing as human beings, especially when it comes to faith. Our mercurial emotions constantly war with our reason. Kicking into faith mode when our emotions or the gravity of a situation leaves us struggling is tough. Like an army preparing for battle, we have to make sure our reason has plenty of backing. We can fortify with prayer and scripture, and consult good strategists. We can read about other people who had great faith, like the patriarch, Abraham, or Corrie Ten Boom. For most, faith doesn't come easy. But we can find comfort in knowing that even when we are wavering, God is greater than our changeable hearts, and he knows everything.

Faith mode is safe mode when
our emotions are off line.

God is greater than our hearts,
and he knows everything.

1 JOHN 3:20

I have always depended on
the kindness of strangers.

An Old Woman and
a Cardboard Box

A young man was in an airport, collecting his bags after a long international flight. He was exhausted and ready to head off to his next destination. As he picked up his last bag he noticed an old woman, small and slightly bent, waiting patiently for her bags. He saw that she had been standing alone for some time, looking as best she could through the people clamoring for their bags, so the young man asked if he could help. She said yes. As people began to disperse and the field of vision expanded, she said, "Oh, there it is." She pointed to a brown cardboard box. As he approached the carousel, he saw the only identifying marks on the box. Written in black marker were the words Mother Teresa.

That man could easily have taken his bags and moved along. What reward is there in helping a stranger, especially one we've encountered in transit—not even close to where we live? This man had the privilege of helping someone who has given her life to "the least of these." What an experience! Yet we never know, as we travel through life, what effect our assistance may have on another, or just whom we are serving when we stop to help.

◎

Lending a hand along life's journey is never a bad idea.

"The King will answer and say to them,
'Truly I say to you, to the extent that you
did it to one of these brothers of Mine,
even the least of them, you did it to Me.

MATTHEW 25:40 NASB

One kind word can warm three winter months.

 Healing Words

A young woman was new to her job in a large organization. She had some ideas for new ways of advertising their products and spent hours developing them. At a yearly planning meeting, where they were encouraged to brainstorm ideas, she gave her thoughts to the group. Her boss (not a person who would easily give credit to another for fear of turning attention from herself), fairly dismissed the young employee's ideas in front of everyone. After the meeting, the young woman returned to her office, crushed. She considered looking for a new job; how could anyone respect her after she had made such a fool of herself? Toward the end of the day, another employee stopped by her office—a peer of her boss. He said, "You're smart, and you have great ideas. Don't get discouraged. This department can be a hard sell." The young woman was surprised. She couldn't imagine that not everyone felt as if she had made a total buffoon out of herself. She was elated. She could go home and not berate herself all night.

The smallest kind word can totally change someone's perspective about a day, a situation, or about him or herself.

◎

It's never good policy to withhold genuine kindness.

A word aptly spoken is like apples of gold in settings of silver.

PROVERBS 25:11

Hope springs eternal in the human breast.

Anticipation—Making Us Wait

The woman who desires more than anything to meet someone special and get married, the couple who wishes they could have a child, the person who is waiting to hear back from a company after an interview—life is filled with occasions to wait. The waiting can be excruciating, even all consuming, especially with the larger life issues.

It's been said that anticipation is half the fun of arriving at the destination. (Depending on the destination, it might be most all of the fun.) Instead of allowing the waiting to consume us and steal our peace of mind and happiness, we would do well to look at the anticipation as part of the overall experience. No matter what we're trying to accomplish, we're living life in the process, living out days that we will never have again. This doesn't mean disregarding sadness and disappointment, but it does mean doing all we can to live and enjoy the days we have leading up to the fulfillment of our desires. It is also wise to bear in mind that once our goal or desires are fulfilled, we are still the same people living (in most cases) the same life. Events don't magically transform life and bring happiness—real transformation happens in small steps over time as we mature and develop in our walk with God.

Don't give away the present
while pining for a future
event or destination.

If we hope for what we do not yet have,
we wait for it patiently.

ROMANS 8:25

Growth is the only evidence of life.

Reunion News

The thought of a high school reunion is exhilarating to some and frightening to others. Each of these reactions can come for a variety of reasons. Some loved high school and would like nothing better than to see old friends and catch up—or to recapture some "glory days." Some people wish to flaunt their success. Others don't attend because they don't feel successful enough. A person might want to show off a svelte figure—or may not want to show a growing waistline or diminishing hair. Truth be told, for most, reunions are more about appearance than substance.

No matter how we feel about reunions, the announcement of one marks time: 10, 20, 30 years have passed. As we look back at the person we were years back, hopefully, we are different.

As we grow older, we mature into the knowledge that the externals don't measure success: job, bank account, house or car. It is measured by our personal development, growth in our spiritual lives and the depth of our personal relationships. Whether you're stoked or stymied by the thought of a reunion, use the announcement as a time to evaluate your life, a time to ask yourself, "Am I living for appearance or reality?"

⊚

**Enjoy reunions, if you dare,
but take time to think
about why you are—
or aren't—there.**

*When I was a child, I talked like a child,
I thought like a child, I reasoned like a child.
When I became a man,
I put childish ways behind me.*

I CORINTHIANS 13:11

Push on—keep moving.

The Lake

Have you ever noticed how the water in a lake keeps moving? Even when the wind is barely blowing, you can still see ripples moving gently across the surface—keeping the water from becoming stagnant.

Sometimes when the cares of life weigh us down and the wind that normally fills our sails dies down, we want to stop moving altogether. Pressures at work and home can seem like more than we can handle. If we're not careful, we can find ourselves slowing down and heading towards stagnation.

During those times, we would be wise to consider the peaceful, ever-moving currents on a lake. When life gets us down, we need to keep moving, even if it's simply to put one foot in front of the other. When you feel overwhelmed, choose to act—even if it seems small or insignificant. Take inventory of how your life is going, and make a list of things that are stifling your inertia. Make another list of what might be done to help you want to get back into a comfortable rhythm. If you're really stumped—seek professional or lay counsel. Whatever you do—keep moving.

◎

Sometimes all we need are adjustments to priorities, or our approach to life, to help jump-start our momentum.

One thing I do: Forgetting what is behind and straining toward what is ahead, I press on.

PHILIPPIANS 3:13-14

We must learn to explore all the
options and possibilities that confront us
in a complex and rapidly changing world.

Concerted Success

Why is it, when it comes to achieving success, some people seem to have it all and others have to work so hard to catch the smallest break? Sure, some of this is dumb luck—right place, right time scenario. If we were to look deeper into the circumstances surrounding one's apparent success, we would most likely find some other essential characteristics.

Retired General (now Secretary of State) Colin Powell is someone who, while not a high achiever in school, put in the time and effort in his jobs despite outside distractions, blatant racism, or working in positions for which he was under-qualified. He maintained focus and got notice. He is also widely known, both in military situations and in his personal life, for employing a tactic that has been key to his success. It has become so typical for him that it is now known as the Powell doctrine—focus, restraint, evaluation, and then decisive action. When faced with a situation, great or small, Powell hesitates. Before every step he takes time to think, evaluate, and plan—and then he proceeds without reserve. No matter what our personal or career goals, that pattern of approach can only help us to lead more productive, successful lives.

⊚

Precede decisive action
with concerted focus.

God hath not given us the spirit of fear;
but of power, and of love, and of a sound mind.

2 TIMOTHY 1:7 KJV

An honest man's word is as good as his bond.

The Truth About Lies

If we were to step back and evaluate the most popular sit-coms on TV today, especially those geared toward 20- and 30-somethings, we'd see that many of the episodes revolve around distortion of the truth. Sure, it's funny when we, the viewers at home, are "in the know" about a situation and see it played out. At times, a series of lies begin to unravel and the perpetrator faces consequences. Most of the time, though, the person is simply sorry to have been discovered in the center of the sticky web. Do these self-absorbed characters ever learn? Usually, by next episode, they're at it again.

Distortion of truth or all-out lies can make for funny plot twists, but when continually offered by the stars of popular shows as the way to react when caught in an unfavorable situation, this behavior begins to seem normal. Our present culture seems to have less and less opposition to lying. But lying is wrong. Accepting it in small ways will only lead to farther-reaching lies. In making lying acceptable, we create a culture of people who don't want to deal with the hard stuff of life and who forsake personal responsibility. Not looking at things for what they are—now that's the most destructive lie of all.

The impact of real-life lies doesn't stop when the episode is over.

Lord, who may dwell in your sanctuary?
Who may live on your holy hill?
He whose walk is blameless and who does what
is righteous, who speaks the truth from his heart.

PSALM 15:1-2

Good company and good discourse
are the very sinews of virtue.

Making Time to Spend

Some couples or friends realize that they haven't had a decent conversation—for months. They don't really know how the other person is doing or how the relationship is going. It's easy for people to coexist and not really communicate. That's one reason why it's good to break away from the normal routines of home and work and get out, even if just for a short time. Leave the house and the ringing telephone, the laundry, and all the other tasks that await us in our domiciles. Whether we are married or single, it is often when we are out with our partner or a good friend that we have our best conversations. As much as it's important to step away and enjoy the company of another with our minds unfettered, it can also be tough to work it into the schedule or budget to go out to a restaurant.

Don't use cost or busyness as reasons not to get out and visit with someone who's important to you. Hit an inviting coffee shop, grab dessert, or get an inexpensive breakfast at a favorite greasy spoon. If it works, make it a tradition, so you can be sure to reserve some time to really get back in touch with someone who's important.

@

The deepest communication
often happens outside
the place where we live.

Be devoted to one another in brotherly love.

ROMANS 12:10

He has a heart, and gets his speeches by it.

More than Words

Many of the retail stores we shop today employ young people, mostly teenagers. As standard procedure, a good number of these clerks have been coached to greet customers with "Hello, did you find everything you needed today?" and to dismiss customers with "Have a nice day." A good lot of teenagers don't think perky enthusiasm is cool—or they feel awkward about interacting with customers on this level. Now an overly ebullient greeting can be a little much to handle, but there's nothing so uninspiring as a clerk of any age delivering their in-store greeting in a deadpan voice that one would use, say, to deliver some bit of bad news. These clerks are doing what they've been told to do, but it's obviously void of substance and, therefore, impact. We would rather hear nothing at all.

The same principle holds true with all that we say. If our words, whether niceties, compliments or general proclamations, aren't backed by sincerity, then they won't be taken to heart. This is not to say that every greeting toward a stranger should be like a reunion of old friends. That is insincere. But in order to be taken seriously, our sentiments must match our words.

For best results, head, mouth
and heart should consult on
a minute-by-minute basis.

On the contrary, in Christ we speak
before God with sincerity.

2 CORINTHIANS 2:17

I would help others, out of a fellow-feeling.

Putting Others First

A TV advertisement features a beautiful woman touting her hair color product. She claims that her brand will leave her hair lustrous and silky for longer than other products. It may be a little more expensive, she says, but *she's worth it.* The message sent by this ad—and a great many others—is "I deserve it." We live in a culture of entitlement. People believe they are entitled to drive certain cars, have particular possessions, and have control over *their* time. Certainly, there is nothing wrong with having nice things, but the attitude of entitlement regarding material things we "deserve" can spill over into other areas of our lives. It's a way of thinking that says, "Me first."

In the book of Matthew, Christ has something unorthodox to say about our possessions and a "me first" mentality. He says, "If someone strikes you on the right cheek, turn to him the other also. And if someone wants to sue you and take your tunic, let him have your cloak as well" (vs. 38-39). If we work hard, it's natural and right to enjoy the results of diligence. But we must not forget the admonition to put others ahead of ourselves and our possessions—and not just our friends, but also our enemies.

@

Put people before pursuits.

Do nothing from selfishness or empty conceit,
but with humility of mind regard one another
as more important than yourselves.

PHILIPPIANS 2:3 NASB

A man should never be ashamed to own
he has been in the wrong, which is but
saying, . . . that he is wiser
today than he was yesterday.

 # Golf Imitates Life

Golf is one of the all-time favorite sports of Americans. Even the busiest executive will often carve out time to relax and test his skill on carpets of green dotted with eighteen elusive holes.

A preacher once said, "You'll never be a great golfer unless you're willing to post a high score." Clearly, the goal in golf is to post the lowest possible score. But what the preacher is driving at is that you can't let yourself become defeated because you hacked up the course on a given day. You have to be willing to admit you still have things to learn about the intricacies of your golf game if you want to become a better player.

That's true of the game of life as well. No one likes to make mistakes, but all of us have days when we hack up the course of our lives and feel like throwing a tantrum and quitting. Those are the times when we need a wise pro to come alongside and say, "Don't give up—look at your mistakes and *learn* from them."

⊚

Don't be so afraid of making mistakes
that you stop trying to become
a better player in the game of life.

*Humility and the fear of the Lord bring
wealth and honor and life.*

PROVERBS 22:4

Speech is a mirror of the soul;

as a man speaks, so is he.

Get to the Point

A man was sitting on a bench in a mall, reading a paper. A man sat next to him, looked around and said quietly, "Hey, you, you interested in making some extra money?" The first man said, "Yeah, sure. Tell me about it." The quiet man said, a bit nervously, "I'll have to come to your house and tell you all about it." So they set up an appointment.

The quiet man arrived at the other man's house right on time. He began to talk. And he talked, but despite the other man's subtle inquiries, the quiet man didn't reveal his scheme. Finally, after an hour had passed, a third man leaped up from behind the couch. The quiet man nearly jumped out of his skin. The man from behind the couch said, "For crying out loud, this guy's harmless." It was an undercover detective. The homeowner had alerted him to the quiet man's supposed moneymaking scheme. The detective had decided to stake out the scene. Turns out, the quiet man was just getting started in a pyramid marketing business. Being the nervous type, he simply could not get to the approach. In matters of business or life, approach determines so much of how we, and the words we speak, will be received.

@

A direct approach usually
insures a better landing.

Show integrity, seriousness and soundness
of speech that cannot be condemned.
TITUS 2:7-8

It is with narrow-souled people as with narrow-
necked bottles; the less they have in them
the more noise they make in pouring out.

Not Like Them

There's a parable about a Pharisee who is so convinced of his good behavior that he prays for all within earshot to hear, "Thank you God that I don't steal or cheat on my wife or take money that isn't due me—like this tax collector, here." Pharisees were a Jewish sect that was zealous for religion, and even more so for display of outward correctness.

It's easy to scoff at the absurdity of such a public proclamation of self-confidence. But in reality, it's easy to fall into the comparison trap. Do you ever find yourself thinking, "Well, I may not be a saint, but at least I give to charity .

. . or I'm faithful to my mate . . . or I don't drink excessively?" The truth is that we all have strengths and weaknesses. What may be a temptation to you may not be a temptation to someone else and vice versa.

It's best to have the mindset of the guilty, but humble, tax collector who would not even look up to heaven, but beat his chest and said, "God have mercy on me." The happy ending states, "This man, rather than the other, went home justified before God."

◉

Resist the urge to build yourself up by exaggerating the faults of others while minimizing your own.

From heaven the Lord looks down and sees all mankind; . . . he who forms the hearts of all, who considers everything they do.

PSALM 33:13, 15

Know thyself.

Getting to Know You. . . .

Four friends would get together and play cards. Mr. Fun liked to play, yes, for the fun of it. Somewhat serious about the game, he more liked the idea of getting together with buddies and "yukking it up." Ms. Right was concerned with everyone following the rules of the game, keeping it moving ahead and on the level. Mr. Myway was intent at winning the game and often reacted with overly strong emotion. Ms. Easy couldn't care less about the game, winning or losing, and enjoyed hanging out. She would sometimes reveal her hand as she talked. This made Mr. Myway and Ms. Right agitated. Mr. Fun found it comical.

It is thought that there are four basic temperaments: Sanguine (the fun way), Melancholy (the right way), Choleric (my way) and Phlegmatic (the easy way). Each one runs on a continuum, and people normally have characteristics from any or all of the categories. In relationships, opposite temperaments often attract and can enhance, but they also can clash, causing conflict and heartache. Counselors are finding that when people learn about temperaments, a great cosmic light bulb is illuminated. Not every approach and reaction to life can or should be categorized, but understanding our basic make-up and motivations and the way we interact with others can indeed change our lives.

@

Understanding temperaments can take us from thinking people different and therefore wrong to different but perfectly okay.

If the whole body were an eye,
where would the hearing be?
If the whole were hearing,
where would the sense of smell be?

1 CORINTHIANS 12:17 NASB

Henceforth the majesty of God revere;
Fear Him, and you have nothing else to fear.

Companion to Fear

Agoraphobia is the fear of public places. If this condition isn't treated, people who suffer can become paralyzed by fear. Usually agoraphobics can articulate what they fear and where they fear it. Some only know a sense of serious apprehension. Aside from traditional therapy, treatment for this condition may include having a trusted companion accompany the patient on small outings. This companion sticks close by. He doesn't taunt or make light of the disorder, but acts as a support. If the person begins to show any signs of panic and a need to leave the place or situation, the person must comply. This is a means of building trust and allowing for future progress.

Agoraphobia is an extreme manifestation of fear. Yet many people suffer from social anxiety and other fears to a lesser (but no less real) degree. If fear is causing you anxiety or holding you back, know that each of us has a Companion, one who goes with us wherever we go. This

Companion fully understands our fears and tells us to cast all our anxieties on Him. He offers peace, rest, and grace beyond measure. All we must do is trust and lean on Him, and He will help us progress and gain courage to face the future.

@

When fear keeps you from
living to the fullest, look to the
One Who gives fullness to life.

*The LORD is the stronghold of my life—
of whom shall I be afraid?*

PSALM 27:1

History is the essence of innumerable biographies.

Just Ask

Children in a first grade class made up a list of questions that they were to ask to their grandparents (or a great aunt or uncle or older friend) about what life was like for them as children. The designated people were to answer these questions and give or mail the answers back to the students. One mother got the mail and opened the thick letter that had been sent from her parents in Arizona to her son. As she read her parent's answers to the questions, she was amazed. There was so much she didn't know. She immediately called her parents and said, "Hey, how come I never knew any of this?" Her dad replied, "Huh. Well, I guess you never asked."

So many of us have people in our lives, parents, grandparents and the like, who have stories to tell. The stories our elders tell are not only theirs, but ours as well. It is unwise to think that we will always have the opportunity to hear the voices and words of those in our lives, especially our elder relations. The policy here: "Ask and Tell." You will get and give a rich history that you can treasure and pass along to those who follow.

❧

Take the opportunity to know the stories others have to tell.

When I was a boy in my father's house,
still tender, and an only child of my mother.

PROVERBS 4:3

God offers to every mind its choice
between truth and repose.

Choices

A Polish woman named Halina was imprisoned in a Nazi concentration camp. She wasn't Jewish, but a devout Catholic who supported Jews during a time when that was a crime, as most know. Halina had a choice; she could have saved herself, by turning her head or going along with the plan to exterminate the Jewish race, but she didn't. She chose to stand against it, to help save Jewish lives, even if it meant sacrificing her own. Once in the camp, she and the other prisoners were treated abominably. One particularly grueling day, when the yelling of a German soldier had become more than she could bear, she snapped. This tiny young girl turned to the soldier and began to step toward him. She felt a sudden sweep of power she could only attribute to God. She said, "You can try to kill my body, but you will never, ever take my soul." Strangely, instead of retaliating, the soldier stepped away.

Halina is now a US citizen. She is still helping people. She is still rising each morning and asking God for help and strength to face the day. She doesn't have to—after all, she has a choice. On large and small scales, so do we.

◉

Whether or not we feel powerful
in any given situation,
we always carry the
power of personal choice.

Choose for yourselves this day whom you will serve.

JOSHUA 24:15

Remember that man's life lies all
within this present, as 'twere but a
hair's-breadth of time; as for the rest,
the past is gone, the future yet unseen.

Focusing on Your Own Yard

Kids always seem to want to be older. Many single people of marrying age wish to have the stability of marriage. And a whole lot of married people wish they could have the freedom of being single again. Some couples can't wait to have kids—others would give anything to recapture some of the old carefree lifestyle. There must be something hard-wired into people that causes them to look ahead, to desire something other than their present lives or situations as the ones they would really like to be in.

We've all heard the adage, "The grass is always greener on the other side." Many of us spend such a great amount of time craning our heads toward our neighbor's "grass," that we don't tend or even see the beauty of our own yards (so to speak). If we're not giving attention to our own yards, then their beauty might just fade. What would happen if we decided to try to find contentment right where we are—in our present situations? What if we gave as much attention to tending the present as we do wishing for something different? Get out the lawnmower and try it.

The grass always looks
greener from a distance.

Not that I speak in respect of want:
for I have learned, in whatsoever
state I am, therewith to be content.

PHILIPPIANS 4:11 KJV

Give us grace and strength
to forbear and to persevere.

Shoring up the Mind

A young woman suddenly experienced a problem with her sight, light flashes, and blurred vision. It didn't worry her—until she began to feel overly fatigued and numb in one hand. She consulted a doctor and, after a battery of tests, was diagnosed with multiple sclerosis. She and her husband were devastated, but she determined to take care of herself and give it a fight. She tried an experimental drug; it suppressed the symptoms, but it robbed her of sleep. This woman, despite all her efforts, could not catch a wink of shut-eye. After time, she could barely function. She wanted to read her Bible but found it impossible to concentrate.

After time and experimentation, she could sleep. The young woman reflected, "Through that experience, I realized that I hadn't memorized Scripture as I should have. I needed to be able to flip to the 'Scripture file' in my brain and find some words of hope and strength. Instead, the file was empty." The Bible is a penetrating and powerful source of help—it is the wellspring of life. Drink deep while you have the strength. When you are weak, the words will lift your spirit, strengthen your heart, and soothe your soul.

◎

God's Word is the wellspring
of the heart, soul and mind.

I meditate on your precepts and consider your ways.
I delight in your decrees; I will not neglect your word.
Psalm 119:15-16

The goal is completing the process.

Living Beyond Face Value Mentality

So much of what we see on TV and in the lives of people we know we see at face value. And, as such, we are often quick to assume that what we see at face value came easily. Advertisements show instant improvements: "I lost 50 pounds in one month on the such-and-such plan," or "I made thousands of dollars in one month doing X." This instant achievement mentality pervades our society. And when we slip into this mentality, no matter how well meaning we are, it's difficult to stay motivated toward what we wish to accomplish.

If we were to look further, beyond face value, we would no doubt have a few revelations. Drawing conclusions about people at face value rarely leads to an accurate picture. Very few people lose weight permanently without a consistent change of eating and physical habits. Get-rich-quick schemes can't compare to diligent financial planning and money management. We must not fool ourselves into looking at our own lives at face value either. In order to achieve what we want, in order to live honestly and productively, we must live according to the principle: the real accomplishment is in planning and staying with every step of the process to achieve it.

❧

What looks too good to be true,
usually is—for everyone else
and for us, too.

Perseverance must finish its work,
so that you may be mature and complete,
not lacking anything.

JAMES 1:4

131

My goal is God Himself, not joy, nor peace,
Nor even blessing, but Himself, my God;
Tis His to lead me there, not mine, but His—
At any cost, dear Lord, by any road.

Making Your Mark

A young writer was attending a series of workshops, culminating with the "how to get published" seminar. Through the series, she became friendly with one of the writers, an older published author. She told the author that she wanted more than anything to have a book published—to see her name on the cover, for other people to know that she was published. She asked him if he thought that a bad ambition.

The instructor told her that certainly wanting to be published is a fine ambition. He also said something that was more valuable than anything else she had learned at any seminar. He said that, in his experience, while becoming a published author can be a mountaintop experience, sooner or later you'll come back down the mountain to face real life. He told her to make sure her life was grounded in things that have real meaning—like relationships, serving others and growing spiritually. Fulfilling ambitions can then be icing on the cake.

God has given all of us gifts that we should express and develop to the fullest. He has also told us where we need to base the heart of our lives—in loving and serving Him and others. That's where we'll make the mark that counts.

@

**Making a mark on earth is fine—
making a mark that lasts, divine.**

*Humble yourselves, therefore,
under God's mighty hand, that
he may lift you up in due time.*

I PETER 5:6

A person who lives right and is right
has more power in his silence
than another has by his words.

Following Through

We've all heard the saying, "Good intentions aren't good enough." However, it's only as we grow older and experience a little more of what life has to offer that we see the truth to this statement. Take relationships. Do we often "cancel out" on plans we've made? Do we neglect returning telephone calls? Do we say, "We've got to get together," every time we see certain people, but never do it?

Our easy-access, mobile society leads us to make many personal connections—maybe more than in any time in history. Unfortunately, it gives us many ways to have to keep in touch. So how do we take good intentions and turn them into a good reality? First, we must evaluate and speak honestly. Are we over-committed to activities? Are our commitments to friends realistic? Are we setting boundaries with our friendships and sticking with them (i.e. "I'd love to be able to talk on the phone with you for an hour, but I really only have ten minutes to spare"). It's important to prioritize and devote our time accordingly. And if someone's good intentions are getting you down, tell them. Lack of honesty often leads to misunderstanding, bitterness, and lost relationships.

⊚

Don't say it if ya can't do it.

*"Simply let your 'Yes' be 'Yes'
and your 'No, No.'"*

Matthew 5:37

Good, to forgive;

Best, to forget!

Living, we fret;

Dying, we live.

Flinging the Albatross Away

An 86-year-old woman was the quintessential grandma. She was cheerful, baked all sorts of excellent goods, and gave without reserve. Everyone loved her. Those who were close to this woman knew that she had an albatross that she could not seem to shake. It was her ex-husband. When she spoke of him, her pupils would grow to pinpoints, and years of harbored bitterness would infuse her words with venom. It had been forty years since they had been married. Second time around, she married a wonderful, loving man and enjoyed twenty-six years with him. Her ex-husband had died, but her resentment lived on. He had mistreated, neglected, and rejected her. She had every reason to be angry. But this anger had formed a shell over her heart, causing pain, and unhappiness.

This woman's granddaughter gently suggested to her grandma that her ex-husband was still making her miserable and that she needed to forgive the scoundrel. The grandmother said she didn't know how she could. The granddaughter suggested, as a first step, praying to God for help to forgive. After time, wrestling, and much prayer, this grandmother was able to forgive. At 87, unencumbered by bitterness, she became a new woman with a new capacity for love.

◎

Even when we carry deep hurts,
even when anger is justified, if we
can't forgive, we can't truly live.

*If ye forgive men their trespasses,
your heavenly Father will also forgive you.*

MATTHEW 6:14 KJV

137

Behold, we know not anything;
I can but trust that good shall fall,
At last—far off—at last, to all,
And every winter change to spring.

The Heat is On

"It's Hot!" Have you ever noticed how, in the middle of a seething summer, people tend to state the obvious? As if saying "It's hot" will somehow cool down the sweltering atmosphere.

Yet focusing on the hovering misery only makes it worse. We'd almost prefer that the weatherman lie to us. Rather than hear, "It's gonna be an eyebrow-singeing scorcher," we'd prefer to hear, "It's gonna be a warm, summer day—here are some great ways to stay cool!" And then we hope Mr. Weatherman can offer some truly helpful tips.

There are seasons in our lives that are like hot, summer days. Sometimes the heat of hard circumstances can seem almost unbearable—like the blazing sun bearing down on a treeless field in July. We seek desperately for even a bit of shade and a few wisps of breeze to bring momentary comfort. We lean on friends who actively help us stay cool rather than point out the heat index.

Thank God we can count on the winds of change in the fall to bring relief from summer heat. In the same way we can count on God to bring relief from the heat of hard circumstances. It's been said that "nothing lasts forever," and that's good a thing to keep in mind when the heat is on.

@

When things get hot, think cool
and know that heat waves pass.

*There is a time for everything, and a season
for every activity under heaven:
a time to weep and a time to laugh,
a time to mourn and a time to dance.*

ECCLESIASTES 3:1, 4

Experience is the name everyone
gives to their mistakes.

Efface Yourself

The attendees at a conference for professional speakers were introducing themselves and saying what kinds of topics they spoke on. One gentlemen said, "I'm an expert on motivating people to achieve their goals." A young woman said, "I'm a health and fitness guru." An older woman said, "I make mistakes. I give talks on how to learn things the hard way!" she ended with a smile. Everyone in the room laughed at the woman's remarks and the atmosphere took on a whole new air of relaxation. Although each speaker indeed had valuable gifts and skills to share, underneath it all everyone realized that like the older woman, they too had made many mistakes along the road to success.

What set the woman apart from the crowd was her humble courage in admitting her shortcomings. She later described the joy and satisfaction of helping others to feel better about themselves by removing the stigma of "not having it all together." Do you feel the pressure of keeping up appearances? Realize that everyone makes mistakes and look for friends and mentors who are comfortable with their flaws as well as their gifts.

◎

Appearances are just what
they are—face-value appearance.
The real living happens in the essence.

*Humble yourselves before the Lord,
and he will lift you up.*

JAMES 4:10

141

Keep your sunny side up.

Singing in the Rain

"Into every life a little rain must fall," is a common saying that is all too true. The important thing to ask ourselves is, "How will I react when the rain clouds gather overheard?"

Do you remember seeing Gene Kelly in the classic movie, "Singing in the Rain?" His irresistible smile stretched across his face as he tap-danced, umbrella in hand underneath the pouring rain. He twirled 'round lampposts while skipping down waterlogged cobblestone avenues, singing his heart out.

It's okay to feel frustrated or have a good cry when life's irritations and challenges pour down on you. But after letting off some emotional steam, we would do well to follow in the foot "taps" of Mr. Kelly: Don a raincoat, some tap shoes, and a smile. In other words, rather than give in to cloudy depression, be determined to put on a sunny disposition—focusing on every ray of sunshine that manages to make its way through the darkening clouds.

Ask God to put a song in your heart on rainy days (or even monsoon seasons). And remember the words of a famous curly-haired redhead from Broadway, "The sun'll come out tomorrow."

*

When you're "stuck with a day that's gray and lonely," try and "pick up your chin and grin."

The rain came down, the streams rose, and the winds blew and beat against that house; yet it did not fall, because it had its foundation on the rock.

MATTHEW 7:25

143

Speak to me as to thy thinkings.

The Gelatin Story

In the Newton house, there is a family tale that is sure to live on for generations. It's the "gelatin story." It's a yarn that's told to every guest who has any meal in their house when the guest is asked if he or she would like a second helping of something. It's the father's story, taken from an experience he had when he was a child. It goes like this:

As a young boy, the father had stopped by a friend's house to see if the friend wanted to play. It was a warm summer night, and the family was just finishing dinner. For dessert, the mom took out a bowl filled with glimmering, brightly-colored, fruited gelatin. The mother said, "Young man, would you like some gelatin?" The boy, trying to be polite, said, "Oh, no thank you." The boy, however, really did want some gelatin. He was just waiting for the second request, the "Oh, c'mon, have some gelatin." But the second request never came. So he sat, wishing and hoping and longing for a bowl of gelatin that never would be.

The moral of the story: Manners and courtesy ring true. Superficial niceties ring false—and, worst of all, can leave you bereft of a dessert.

Whether in the board room
or the dining room,
speak from the heart.

"*Let your statement be,
'Yes , yes ' or 'No, no ';
anything beyond these is of evil.*
MATTHEW 5:37 NASB

It was a high counsel that I once
heard given to a young person,
"Always do what you are afraid to do."

Garden Tours

The woman couldn't believe she had received the
assignment. "The only thing I've ever grown is a pinto
bean in a paper cup in kindergarten." Although she was
ecstatic at the prospect of writing an article for a well-
known magazine, it was tempting to fall prey to
the self-defeating thoughts in her
mind, whispering all her inadequa-
cies and inexperience.

In a moment of epiphany,
she called out to God in silent
prayer, "Lord, You wouldn't
have given me the privilege of
writing this assignment if You
didn't intend to equip me to do
it—and to do it well. Please give
me the faith to take one step at a

time and the mental strength to silence the voices that are taunting my mind." She then went to work. She contacted gardening experts and became a quick study on elements that ensured a standout garden tour. She attended tours and the beauty of flowers and the dedication of avid gardeners inspired her. In the end, she wrote a professional article displaying some of the best tours in the southeast. Do you want to try something new, but are plagued by feelings of inadequacy? Ask God to remove your fear and replace it with faith.

@

Remove the barriers of fear by knocking them down with faith.

"My grace is sufficient for you, for my power is made perfect in weakness."

2 CORINTHIANS 12:9

Children have more need of models than critics.

Fathering the Fatherless

Today, with half of all marriages ending in divorce, single-parent homes are commonplace. As hard as many single parents work for their children, these children don't always have the support and guidance they need. This is especially true when it comes to spending time with an adult who is a positive role model. The single-parent situation, along with other factors, has led to a growing lack of respect for authority, increased violence, and apathy among young people.

One man in Rhode Island saw all of these symptoms played out with the children in his community. He wanted to do something but didn't know what. He read a book about children and the absolute necessity for positive role models, and it made a big impression on him. He began to volunteer as a Big Brother to a nine-year-old boy who didn't have a father. They attended sporting events and just "hung out" and talked. This man says it's the best thing he's ever done with his free time, that he can already see the difference he has made. Kids are precious and impressionable.

Whether it's volunteering through an organized program or being there for kids from single-family homes of people we know, we all have the opportunity to make a difference.

◎

Reaching out to a child of
a single parent, even for
one event or occasion, can make
an impression that lasts a lifetime.

Religion that God our Father accepts
as pure and faultless is this:
to look after orphans and
widows in their distress.

JAMES 1:27

149

Tell me with whom thou art found
And I will tell thee who thou art.

Staying in the Race

A man entered his old, swayback mule into the Kentucky Derby. The gray-haired, shaggy beast of burden, his belly almost dragging the ground, stood in stark contrast to the sleek muscle-bound thoroughbreds. The jockeys protested, "This isn't right!" The owner of the mule responded, "Well, of course I don't intend for him to win, I just thought the exposure would do him some good."

Sometimes our lives can resemble a swayback, droopy-bellied mule. Maybe we're feeling worn down or worn out and in need of inspiration. In such times, it's vital to recognize when we've gotten off track and have the courage to take steps to get back on course. Exposing ourselves to caring people, churches, and seminars that will revive our tired souls is a great way to fuel our determination to continue striving to become the kind of person we want to be. Often we can find the encouragement to move beyond our mistakes and pain if we can connect with others who have traveled a similar path. We may just need to push ourselves out of a rut and into the running.

@

When you're like a tired, old mule
in the race of life, surround
yourself with thoroughbreds.
"The exposure might do you some good."

Throw off everything that hinders and the sin
that so easily entangles, and let us run with
perseverance the race marked out for us.

HEBREWS 12:1

Our hearts, our hopes, our prayers, our tears,
Our faith triumphant o'er our fears,
Are all with thee—are all with thee!

Denial & Faith

Where does denial end and faith begin? Really, what's the difference between faith and denial? Should we just put on a plastic smile and go on about our lives as if we are totally unaffected by circumstances that are reeling out of control?

Let's face it, when a teenager comes home past curfew, or a blood test indicates an abnormality, or a job is lost—we are going to have strong feelings about it. When we are experiencing difficult circumstances, especially long-term situations, we are not going to be able to face them with grace every moment of every day. We can hope to, strive to, desire to live with grace, but we are but mortals. That's where faith comes in. Faith is not denial. *Faith* is when you choose to focus on God's ability to see you through in spite of your feelings. *Denial* is when you stifle your feelings and put on a facade of invincibility. We can focus on our predicaments, or on God's provision.

Feelings of anxiety are a natural part of the human condition. Ask God to help you move through your feelings to find faith that He will be there when you need Him.

Faith is a matter of focus.

Without faith it is impossible to please him:
for he that cometh to God must believe
that he is, and that he is a rewarder
of them that diligently seek him.

HEBREWS 11:6 KJV

Routines beg, from time to time,
careful evaluation.

The Coffee Cup Routine

A man and wife had been married twenty-five years. Being New Englanders, they had many routines, one of which was to have breakfast together every morning. The man was more reserved, but mischievous. The wife was talkative. One day, while the woman was talking, the man held out his coffee cup. She, without thinking, took the cup, poured coffee into it, and returned it to him. (In the past, he had always asked or poured it himself.) The next day, he did the same thing. She again took it, filled it, and returned it to the table. The man did this every day for nearly one year with the same results. One day, he held out his cup, she took it, and he began to laugh. "What are you laughing for?" she asked. He revealed his routine. From that day on, he became the official "coffee pourer"—for both of them.

This is a comical example of the way in which we slip into routines. Sometimes these patterns are good and help us keep with the rhythm of life. But sometimes our patterns of behavior or speech can be destructive. We would do well to step back and evaluate the patterns in our relationships—what and why we do and say the things we do.

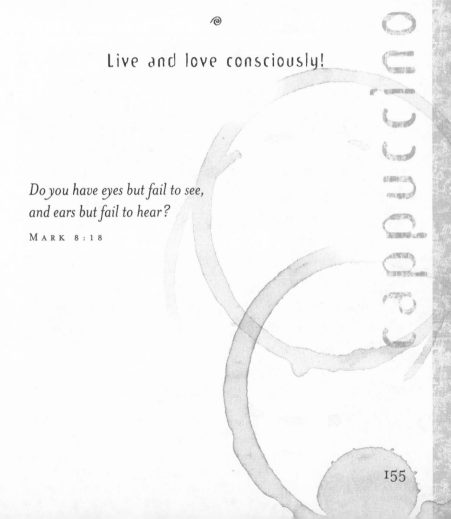

Live and love consciously!

Do you have eyes but fail to see,
and ears but fail to hear?

MARK 8:18

155

The first rule is to keep an untroubled spirit.
The second is to look things in the face
and know them for what they are.

Eyes Wide Open

We hear it so often, after a relationship has crumbled, or a job or project is lost. "When I look back, I can see where things started to go wrong. . . . " It's the old "hindsight is 20/20" coming into play. Why is that? Why can't we see things clearly while we're in the midst of the circumstances?

Some might say that we don't see them because we *don't want* to see them . . . we want the relationship to work or the situation to last. We don't want to put a damper on a present enjoyment—must not disrupt things. Whether we really can't see the truth in our relationships or circumstances, or we're ignoring the warning signs, if these things continue, we can end up with a serious mess.

We can't always recognize things when we're right in the thick of them, but we can take steps to live more honestly.

A first step is praying for God to show us truths about our life and relationships. He sees everything as it really is, and He promises wisdom to those who ask. And we can purpose to live with our eyes open, even if it's hard to look our lives "in the face." If we do that, we won't have to take months or years to sort out the muck of things that are left when we live with our eyes closed.

Stop, look and listen to warning signs— and then take steps to address them.

O great and powerful God . . .
Your eyes are open to all the ways of men.

JEREMIAH 32:18, 19

Every human being is intended to have
a character of his own; to be what no
others are, and to do what no other can do.

Different Strokes

We often smile sheepishly when we hear the old adage, "Opposites attract!" We may even laugh as we contemplate couples of contrast such as the Odd Couple—the classic embodiment of Mr. Neat Orderly vs. Mr. Messy Chaos. The contrast can make even the most open-minded person shake his head at the mystery of such relationships.

The Felix Ungers of the world go about their daily routines with meticulous care and feeding, while the Oscar Madisons fill their days with carefree abandon, munching hot dogs all the while. The Felix Ungers have bedrooms and offices that mother would be proud of, while the Oscar Madisons can't even open the doors to their bedrooms or offices for fear of toppling a cascading mound of "stuff."

It's only natural to see life through our own eyes and experiences. Our own perspectives are all we have to go on—until we purpose to look at life through the eyes and experiences of someone else. Even if we don't fully agree with or understand another person's point of view or paradigm, we should seek to respect differences rather than belittle them—we may just prove once again that opposites attract.

❡

Try to take on another's perspective on life, and it might just change yours for the better.

"Treat others the same way you want them to treat you.

LUKE 6:31 NASB

Business, you know, may bring money,
but friendship hardly ever does.

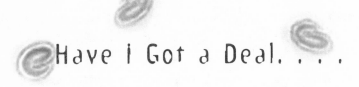

Have I Got a Deal. . . .

A woman answered her telephone to find a young man on the other line. It was Chip, a young man they had met recently. He asked if her husband was home. The woman said he wasn't and asked if she could leave a message. Chip, in a nervous voice, asked, "Well, uh, I have this, uh, opportunity. Do you, uh . . . do you know anyone who would like to make a few thousands of extra dollars, uh, each month?" The woman, trying to contain her laughter, said, "Well, Chip, I don't right off hand, but if I do, I'll sure let you know." He seemed perplexed, thanked her, and then abruptly said good-bye.

The well-meaning young man had obviously become involved in a pyramid business and wished to pass on the opportunity. Pyramid businesses work for some people— but many of the people in these businesses threaten their friendships with their desire to share that opportunity. What's more, when the business people approach friends, the friends can feel that they are merely sitting ducks for a business presentation, that their friends' motives aren't genuine. When mixing business and friendship, always take care—your relationship is more important than any business opportunity—even if it could mean a few thousands of extra dollars each month.

@

Business plans are not the plans we should make with friends.

Love must be sincere . . .
Honor one another above yourselves.

ROMANS 12:9-10

Laughter is the corrective force, which
prevents us from becoming cranks.

Abe-le to Laugh

Sometimes life can feel very serious: a friend has emer-
gency surgery, an unexpected bill arrives in the mail,
or an older parent begins a physical or mental decline.
There are myriads of elements in life that we cannot
control; and it's easy to become anxious and lose our joy.

Interestingly, a man who seemingly had the weight of the
world on his shoulders during the Civil War, had this to
say about coping with the seriousness of life: "With the
fearful strain that is on me night and day, if I did not
laugh I should die." You guessed it—those are the words of
one of the most beloved presidents of our time—Abraham
Lincoln. Even President Lincoln realized that laughter
can be therapeutic. It can provide both an emotional and
physical lift—we can literally feel the stress escaping from
our bodies as we let loose with a belly laugh. Better yet, are
the times we laugh to the point of tears!

Laughter may not take our problems away, but it certainly alleviates some of our anxiety. Watch your favorite funny movies; get together with friends who have a sense of humor, and lighten up at every possible opportunity.

◉

Life's load is lifted with laughter.

A cheerful heart is good medicine, but
a crushed spirit dries up the bones.

PROVERBS 17:22

A man of genius makes no mistakes.
His errors are volitional and
are the portals of discovery.

Living With Mistakes

"I can't believe I did that!" How many times have you made this declaration to yourself after making a mistake? It is so easy to fall into a self-loathing pity party when we don't measure up to our expectations or the expectations of others. Sometimes we say things we wished we had not, or we miss an important appointment or engagement, and sometimes we even break our promises. These kinds of mistakes—as well as a million pitfalls at work, home, and leisure—can make us feel like failures from time to time.

The truth is that no one likes to make mistakes—yet everyone makes them. So how did making mistakes get such a bad reputation? Ask any optimist and he will tell you that your mistakes can be your best teachers. He will also tell you that what separates a growing person from one who is stagnant is the ability to learn from mistakes rather than wallow in them. The next time you "blow it," "miss it," or "foot-in-mouth-it" big time, ask yourself, "Why did that happen?" Then ask, "How can I avoid making this same mistake again?" Then take responsibility, make adjustments, and keep moving forward.

෧

Learn from your mistakes,
but leave them behind
as you move ahead.

I lift up my eyes to the hills—
where does my help come from?
My help comes from the Lord.

PSALM 121:1-2

An invasion of armies can be resisted,
but not an idea whose time has come.

Brain Storms

A four-year-old child draws a picture for her dad with her collection of crayons. The picture shows her dad, a green and purple stick figure, complete with a bright orange necktie, working at his desk. She can't wait to show it to him. The minute he walks through the door she bursts forward, picture extended for him to see. He, of course, gives the picture glowing reviews.

Remember how it felt when you were a child and you drew a picture or made something and presented it to someone for approval? Do you remember the sound of your heart beating wildly with the hope that the recipient would approve of your creation?

Often times as adults we still have those heart-pounding experiences when we are sharing an idea with someone. Our minds warn us, "They may not like it! They may think it's a dumb idea!" Yet something within us yearns to share the idea and see what possibilities may lay ahead. If you or a friend have an idea for a creative or meaningful get-together, an easier way to accomplish something, or a business concept, encourage each other. Half the fun is exploring new possibilities and sharing the excitement that "It just might work!"

◈

Be kind to the ideas of others—
and find people who will
be kind to yours.

*Encourage one another
and build up one another.*

1 THESSALONIANS 5:11 NASB

167

Polly, put the kettle on, we'll all have tea.

Coffee, Tea and "We"

The English have an enviable tradition of enjoying afternoon tea with friends and family. Silver teapots filled with Earl Grey, silver trays displaying raspberry scones and lemon curd—these make up the familiar sights and sounds of a traditional English tea.

What a lovely way to get off of life's carousel for a time to re-focus on one of the most important things in life—our relationships. There's something incredibly inviting about a coffee and teashop, where the smell of freshly ground coffee beans and hundreds of varieties of loose teas mingle in the air. Soothing jazz or classical music often provides a delectable environment for good conversation and a great opportunity to unwind. Coffee bars and tearooms are springing up all over the country. Why not invite a friend to linger with you over a warm, soothing cup of premium coffee or tea in a relaxed atmosphere? Enjoy the rich rewards of uninterrupted, relaxed conversation and a growing relationship. Growing relationships take time and planning—coffee grounds and tealeaves may just be the best fertilizer of all!

Nothing stimulates the senses like coffee or tea with friends.

Let your conversation be always full of grace.

COLOSSIANS 4:6

A wise friend of mine did usually say,
"That which is everybody's business
in nobody's business."

Running Interference

The word "interfere" stems from the Latin verb ferire, which means "to strike or to wound." Before the early 19th century, the word was commonly used to describe a problem with a horse's gait, when one foot would hit against the opposing foot. Envisioning a trotting horse, we can certainly see where this awkward gait would present some problems—the horse would have a devil of a time trying to move ahead with any bit of stealth or finesse. What frustration for the poor creature—and for the person who wanted the horse as transportation or for sport! This also gives us a picture of what happens when we "interfere," in the modern sense of the word, in the lives and business of other people.

It is important to be honest with people—especially when they ask for advice. But interfering is a horse of another color. When we interfere, in the modern sense of sticking our noses where they don't belong, we serve only to strike and wound, to leave the people we've infringed upon like the awkward horse, unfit to move ahead with stealth or finesse.

⟐

If you would advise, be wise.

Make it your ambition to lead a quiet life,
to mind your own business.

1 THESSALONIANS 4:11

Alas, oh, love is dead!
How could it perish thus?
No one has cared for it:
It simply died of frost.

Penny For Your Thoughts— and Feelings

What human being on the face of the planet wouldn't love to hear the words, "You're fun to be around!" or "Thanks for being such a great friend," or "I can really be myself when I'm with you." Deep down, all of us long to know that we are appreciated—that someone's life is a little better because we're a part of it. Why, then, do we often neglect to tell our friends or colleagues how we feel about them or how they make our daily lives a little (or a lot) better?

The next time your heart is telling you that someone is making a positive impact on your life or simply brightening your day, don't ignore it—let the person know. In addition to telling someone verbally that we appreciate them, there are many other ways to express our thanks: send a cookie bouquet, write a note on quality stationary, buy a card, pick up a token gift, or spring for lunch or dinner. Just as you can't say, "I love you" too many times to your spouse or children, you can't say, "I appreciate you" too often to acquaintances, co-workers, or friends.

The second is like unto it,
Thou shalt love thy neighbour as thyself.

MATTHEW 22:39 KJV

173

For kindness begets kindness evermore.

I Came, I Saw!

We are all familiar with the quotation, "I came, I saw, I conquered." Well, there's a great context in which we can apply the "I came, I saw" part of that quotation to our relationships.

Do you remember as a youngster feeling proud and special when someone came to watch you play ball, perform in a play, or tickle the ivories at a piano recital? As adults, we appreciate the same support in our endeavors. It helps validate our goals and dreams when friends and family members "come and see" the results of hours or years of practice and study.

The next time a friend, family member, or co-worker invites you to a graduation, an art show, or a sporting event that they've put many hours of practice and effort into, try hard to show up and lavish your support. It will be a tremendous morale booster for your friend to know that you care about what they have spent a part of their life pursuing. Remember the importance of being an "I came, I saw" kind of friend and watch your relationships grow exponentially as a result.

◎

It's hard to applaud if
you're not at the event.

Each of you should look not only to your
own interests, but also to the interests of others.

PHILIPPIANS 2:4

'Twixt the optimist and the pessimist
The difference is droll:
The optimist sees the doughnut
But the pessimist sees the hole

Sunny Side Up

The default mode of most people's thinking is negative. Sadly, this is often true. If we're not aware of it, those negative thoughts can easily turn into negative talk—both to ourselves and to others.

If you suspect that you aren't Mr. or Ms. Sunshine, it might be helpful to take an informal personal inventory. Become aware of what you are saying and how you are saying it. Ask yourself some simple questions such as: Do I tend to think encouraging or discouraging thoughts most of the time? Are the first words out of my mouth usually positive or negative?

Most people prefer the company of a naturally optimistic person. If given the choice to be around someone who emits messages like, "You can do it!" and "No problem," wouldn't you choose to surround yourself with that kind of encouragement rather than an Eyeore-type personality who puts a damper on your conversations? If you lean toward the pessimistic side, work at re-training your mind and heart. Negativity feeds negativity. Tack up some positive quotes on your bathroom mirror, and try to spend time with optimistic people. It takes work, but, even if you don't believe it, *you can* be a positive person.

@

Positive thoughts . . .
lead to positive words . . .
lead to positive actions . . .
lead to positive experiences.

Rejoice in the Lord always.
I will say it again: Rejoice!

PHILIPPIANS 4:4

One thing people have in common
is that they are all different.

The Trouble with Clones

"You say To-may-to," I say "To-mah-to." "Different strokes for different folks." "To each his own." These sayings epitomize the melting pot of personalities and relational styles that make up the human race. While differences can become fodder for good-hearted teasing, they can also become a point of conflict if we expect others to conform to our way of thinking or doing things most of the time. (And reality is, they won't.)

Good relationships at work, home, and in social situations are those in which people are sensitive to personality differences and preferences. Consequently, they seek to find compromises that will be enjoyable and beneficial for all involved. The best relationships allow plenty of room for give and take and realize that "variety is the spice of life that gives it all its flavor." Strive to be flexible when possible. Respect and learn from the different qualities and styles of the people around you. Be careful not to insist that your ideas or game plans are always the best. You will open a whole new world of possibilities and gain the admiration of others by including rather than excluding them.

🌀

Without the spice of variety,
life would be a bland affair.

Do everything in love.

1 CORINTHIANS 16:14

179

Courage is often caused by fear.

Facing Down Fear

"I am scared to death." "I am afraid." "I'm not sure if I can do it." In the game show *Jeopardy*, these are "Phrases you wouldn't find in the annals of famous quotations." Admitting fear or uncertainty isn't considered a virtue in American culture. Yet on closer inspection, is it really so bad to admit fear? Isn't it true that what matters is not the admittance of fear, but how one responds to it?

The American Heritage Dictionary defines courage as: *The state or quality of mind or spirit that enables one to face danger, fear, or vicissitudes with self-possession, confidence, and resolution.* Where, then, did we get the notion that admitting fear is somehow cowardly? It may well be linked to the American value of strength in self-sufficiency. But wouldn't we be people of greater character and nobility if we would focus more on building character and spiritual strength instead of on the external appearances of fearlessness? Even the toughest people—high-ranking officials, officers of the law, elite military forces—have fears. The esteemed quotes found in the annals of history come not from those who had no fear, but from those who faced life with self-possession, confidence, and resolution—true courage.

It's not fear, but how
we react to it, that defines
our strength of character.

When I am afraid, I will trust in you.

PSALM 56:3

*Liberality consists less in giving
a great deal than in gifts well timed.*

Tokens

Have you ever been given a small gift simply as a token of appreciation for being you? Didn't it make you feel special? It's amazing how a small or relatively inexpensive gift can reap such big benefits in the hearts of the recipients. Token gifts say, "I thought of you when I saw this and just *had* to buy it for you!" If you're on the receiving end, it's touching to know that you are thought of in the minds and hearts of others as they go about their busy lives.

A great way to facilitate token gift giving is to establish a "friendship budget." Even five dollars per month is a great start to a habit that can bring joy to your friends. If you've established a small budget and have made gift-giving a priority, you'll be prepared to act the next time you see something and think, "So-and-so would *love* this!" You will not have to think twice or talk yourself out of the opportunity to brighten someone's day. Token gifts are a great investment in your relationships. Each time your friend sees or uses your gift, she will be reminded of how much she means to you.

&

A specially chosen, impromptu gift is the best gift of all.

If there be first a willing mind,
it is accepted according to that a man hath,
and not according to that he hath not.

II CORINTHIANS 8:12 KJV

No mind is thoroughly well organized
that is deficient in a sense of humor.

 # Funny Bone

Have you ever been around someone who is so uptight that everyone else in the room feels tense too? It's no barrel of monkeys to be around a person who can't relax in the presence of others and laugh at themselves on occasion. When we make a mistake or something embarrassing happens to us, we have two choices: we can become mortified and excuse ourselves from the room, or we can lighten up and share a laugh with the people around us. *Faux pas* and mishaps are a part of life. In addition, if you can't bring yourself to see the humor in life's pitfalls, you can plan to be regularly embarrassed and stressed-out.

Consider looking at life from a duck's perspective. Ducks have a layer of soft, downy feathers underneath the top feathers that stay dry—calm, cool, collected, because the top feathers have a special oil that protects them. That's how our self-esteem needs to be—calm, cool, collected on the inside while letting mistakes and embarrassments roll off our backs. The love of God and of those who care about us should protect us from becoming bruised when we misstep.

@

When life's mishaps come your way,
make like a duck: give a good natured
quack and let 'em roll off your back.

A happy heart makes the face cheerful,
but heartache crushes the spirit.

PROVERBS 15:13

A faithful friend is a strong defense;
and he that hath found such a one
hath found a treasure.

Buddies & Bad Days

Everyone has a bad day every now and then, but it's tough not to take it personally if your friend or colleague seems out of sorts. Yet part of being a good friend is realizing that all people have bad moments or circumstances that weigh them down from time to time. Most of us also have some level of emotional baggage. And even if the baggage has been dealt with and stowed away, there are times when it can rear its head and make an unexpected and unwelcome appearance. So if your normally bubbly buddy seems to have had some air let out of his or her bubble, realize it's probably not a reflection on you, but simply something your friend is mulling over. If someone you care about seems snappy or just plain unhappy, be a good pal and allow for momentary deviations from the norm. If he is a good friend as well, he will do the same for you when you're feeling blue.

Remember to allow space for human beings to be . . . human. Don't play the heavy when your friend is weighted down—give him the benefit of the doubt and some space too.

Don't add weight by "playing the heavy."

There is a friend who sticks closer than a brother.

PROVERBS 18:24

O fond anxiety of mortal men!
How vain and inconclusive arguments
Are those, which make thee
beat thy wings below.

Time Crunch

Madeline was fastidious about being on time. She prayed aloud before leaving her driveway, "Dear God, *please* let me get to the hotel before 8:30 to set up this presentation without being rushed!" Madeline tooled down the highway, sipping her coffee and humming along with country singers on the radio. Suddenly she realized that she had missed her exit. She banged her fist on the steering wheel in frustration and zoomed off the closest exit.

It was 8:15 by the time Madeline got back on track. She reached the hotel at 8:25, grabbed her laptop, and made a flying leap for the meeting room. She could see her boss waiting at the door and tried desperately to compose herself before greeting him. "The meeting's at 8:30, right? Don't worry, I can set up in a jiffy." Her boss patted her on the shoulder and said, "Relax, we serve coffee at 8:30, but the meeting starts at 9:00." Madeline smiled sheepishly and asked God to forgive her for becoming so upset. *And even if she had been late,* she thought, *would it really have been the end of the world?*

How much anxiety we would save ourselves if we could let the little things be . . . little things.

@

Try to look at the little problems
with the wide-scope lens of
big-picture perspective.

Cast all your anxiety on him
because he cares for you.

1 PETER 5:7

Acknowledgments

The Aprocrypha (8,188), Henry David Thoreau (10,36,90), Colonel Blacker (12), John Dryden (14), William Shakespeare (16,146), George Crabbe (18), Ralph Waldo Emerson (20,126,148), Anonymous (22,72,132,180), John Alexander Joyce (26), Mencuis (28), Julia A. Fletcher Carney (30), George Herbert (32,92), John Greenleaf Whittier (34), John Ruskin (38), George Meredith (40), John Milton (42), Aeschylus (44), Alfred Tennyson (46,56), George MacDonald (48), Marcus Aurelius Antoninus (50), Henry Wadsworth Longfellow (52,154), G. K. Chesterton (54), Socrates (58,120), Diogenes Laertius (60), John Locke (62), Robert Browning (64,138), Thomas Jefferson (66), Tertullian (68), Thomas Cole (70), William Cowper (74,80), Ernest Hemingway (76), Morgan Taylor (78), Sir Thomas Browne (82), Walt Whitman (84), American Proverb (86), Anne Bradstreet (88), Tennessee Williams (94), Japanese Proverb (96), Alexander Pope (98,114,118), John Henry Cardinal Newman (100), Thomas Morton (102), James William Fulbright (104), Miguel De Cervantes (106), Izaak Walton (108,172), Samuel Rogers (110), Robert Burton (112), Publius Syrus (116), James Fordyce (122), Thomas Carlyle (124), Marcus Aurelius (128,158), Robert Lewis Stevenson (130), F. Brooks (134), Phillips Brooks (136), Alfred Lord Tennyson (140), Oscar Wilde (142), Lew Brown (144), Joseph Joubert (150), Johann Wolfgang von Goethe (152), Lily Kent (156), William Ellery Channing (160), Jane Austen (162), Henri Bergson (164), James Joyce (166), Victor Hugo (168), Anonymous Nursery Rhyme (170), Angelus Silesius (174), Sophocles (176), McLandburgh Wilson (178), French Proverb (182), Jean de La Bruyere (184), Samuel Taylor Coleridge (186), Dante (190).

Also available:
Coffee Break Devotions: Latte

If you have enjoyed this book,
or if it has impacted your life,
we would like to hear from you.

Please contact us at:

Honor Books
An Imprint of Cooks Communications Ministries
4050 Lee Vance View
Colorado Springs, CO 80918
Or by e-mail at *www.cookministries.com*